Discover the Language of the Mind

of the Mind

"The Hypnotist's Guide to Psycho-Linguistics"

By Patrick K. Porter, Ph.D.

Foreword by Dr. Paul T. Adams

*This book is dedicated to those wishing
to discover the essence of change technology.
May you awaken to the language of your mind.*

Lifestyle Improvement Centers, LLC

d/b/a Positive Changes Hypnosis
4390 Tuller Road
Dublin, Ohio 43017
614-792-8100

Other Books
By Patrick K. Porter, PhD

*Awaken the Genius – Mind
Technology for the 21st Century
6 Secrets of GENIUS*

For self-help CDs visit our website www.positivechanges.com or www.hypnosistogo.com

Lifestyle Improvement Centers, LLC
d/b/a Positive Changes Hypnosis
4390 Tuller Road
Dublin, OH 43017
Phone: (614) 792-8100
877-POSITIVE

Cover Art: Larry Branham

Revised Edition: Oct 2004/April 2011
First printed under the title *Psycho-Linguistics, The Language of the Mind*: April 1994
(Previous ISBN: 0-9637611-7-X)

ISBN: 0-9761712–0-1
Printed in the United States of America

10 9 8 7 6 5 4 3 2

Table of Contents

FOREWORD

It has often been said that *knowledge is power.* The truth is that knowledge *applied* is power. Through Psycho-Linguistics, Dr. Patrick Porter teaches how to apply the power of mind technology. Patrick Porter has often been noted for his ability to take technical, academic jargon into a laymen's language that is not only practical, but also usable by people from every walk of life. Psycho-Linguistics is perhaps his best display of this skill.

In 1967 I wrote a book called *The New Self-Hypnosis.* Within its pages I wrote about King Solomon who said, in essence, that the thing which determines human character is not what a man thinks or verbalizes consciously, but what he thinks "in his heart," or subconsciously. "For as a man thinketh in his heart, so is he." (Proverbs 23:7 K.J.V.) Since the days of King Solomon, many discoveries about the mind have confirmed what he said. What you think in your heart, or other-than-conscious, becomes you. This can be either good or bad, depending upon how you created the program. At that time I believed (and still do) that the very best way to reach those other-than-conscious programs was through hypnosis and/or self-hypnosis. That was in 1967.

Today, with Dr. Porter's Psycho-Linguistics, access to the other-than-conscious is easier, more concise and more effective than ever before. What Dr. Porter has done in developing Psycho-Linguistics was to blend together the best of hypnosis, visualization and a relatively new science known as Neuro-Linguistic Programming. This is hypnosis at its highest level. He has taken these sciences out of the exclusive domain of academia and into the realm of the practical. Each of these methods has been time-tested for long-term success. Dr. Porter and his associates use these techniques on a daily basis in Positive Changes Hypnosis Centers across North America.

Here are tools that can help the seasoned professional or the neophyte. However, you must do more than simply read the material presented in Psycho-Linguistics; you must apply the teachings. A unique feature of Psycho-Linguistics is that Dr. Porter doesn't just teach you theory. In addition to the methodology, he gives you word-for-word formulas that you can use immediately. Dr. Porter has indeed written a text you can refer to for the rest of your professional career or personal life. You will read it *and apply it* over and over again.

PAUL T. ADAMS, PH.D.

ACKNOWLEDGMENTS

I wish to offer my thanks to the creative force known by some as God, and by others as Divine Mind, for continuous guidance and the motivation to persevere in my educational goals and development as a hypnotist and counselor.

I wish to give thanks to my loving family who supported me through my research and development; especially my wife, Cynthia, who has done such a fine job editing the volumes of information that went into the creation of this text.

I wish to express my thanks to my father, Dr. Michael J. Porter, who started my research in the area of psychology at an early age by teaching me how the power of my mind, through hypnosis and imagery, could transform my life. Special thanks are also due to Dr. Paul T. Adams who allowed me to serve as his apprentice and to develop the skills of Psycho-Linguistics.

I'm also grateful to the staff of NLP of Arizona and NLP Comprehensive who trained me in the skills of NLP. I give special thanks to the founders of NLP, Richard Bandler and John Grinder for bringing forth this non-judgmental therapeutic approach that has proven their philosophy time and again that, *"Anyone can do anything… If one person can do something it is possible to model it and teach it to anyone else."*

I would also like to give thanks to the staff at Light and Sound Research, especially Linnea Ried and Larry Gillen, for allowing me to be a part of the growing field of mind technology. Also, special thanks to Jerry DeShazo, a lifelong student who encouraged my research and development as a hypnotist.

Heartfelt thanks go to Jennifer Severo for demonstrating the Psycho-Linguistics testing and rapport-building procedures throughout this book.

Thanks to all my franchise partners who continue to help improve upon the technology of change. Special appreciation is due the many thousands of clients who have passed through the doors of our Positive Changes Hypnosis Centers, and have allowed me to use and expand upon the approaches outlined in this text.

I would also like to honor all the *"Networkers"* out there who make this world work with such harmony and consistency. A special thanks to Rita Livingston who sponsored my work into Barbados, West Indies where I met with Dr. Jim Hurtak who provided me with the inspiration to put my work into its current format.

Special and heartfelt thanks to the reader. My hope is that one of you will become inspired to create the next exciting mind technology so that I can continue to learn and grow. As a friend of mine, Dr. Gil Gilley, once said, *"When you stop growing, you begin to rot!"* May the ground under your feet be fertile soil and the seeds of greatness sprout through your actions. May you benefit from the years of discovery found in this text.

PATRICK K. PORTER, PH.D

PREFACE

There are many abilities of the mind that we humans have in common. Our minds all process information from a foundation of five primary access systems, better known as our senses. These are visual, auditory, kinesthetic (tactile or emotional feelings), and the senses of smell (olfactory) and taste (gustatory). The five senses help our minds process the world around us. Many will argue over the existence of a sixth sense. The possibility of extra-sensory perception, or a sixth sense, is the topic of considerable controversy. To me, it seems logical that when all five senses are working together in harmony and forecasting a probable future, it creates, in essence, a "sixth sense."

All the senses work together to create your perception of reality. This is not to be confused with reality itself, however. Just ask two eyewitnesses, who were at the same event at the same time, to describe what they saw and heard at the scene. Don't be too surprised when completely different versions are described to you. When touching into the language of the mind, you are dealing with perceptions of reality, or an individual's inner map and guideline, not reality itself.

Perceptions are the guidelines people use to define and achieve personal success. Therefore, success is a state of mind. Through the patterns of Psycho-Linguistics, I have spent the last 18 years researching how to create that successful state of mind; how and when to use the visual and auditory fields, the emotional responses, and, when appropriate, the gustatory and olfactory senses.

In my early years of practice, I felt awkward every time I was asked to explain just how the brain and mind work. I understood it in my own mind, but could never put it into the right words – until the computer age dawned and I found the perfect analogy for the brain and mind.

Just like a computer, the brain (hardware), and mind (software), require programming and specific steps and sequences before you can gain access. Once you have found that access, the only limits are those you set. If you have ever attempted to program a computer, you know exactly what I mean. The computer has certain laws that must be followed exactly, or it will not do the function you wish it to perform. No matter how frustrated or upset you get, a computer will simply wait patiently for you to make a command according to its laws. When you finally learn the laws of the computer, and follow them to the letter, it will happily and effortlessly perform the function you desire.

So it is with the mind. If you attempt to make changes in your life without ever gaining access to the laws that are working in your mind, it will either do nothing at all, or perhaps will bring you an outcome that is much different from the one you had set out to achieve.

My discovery of the mind started at a very early age when I was mastering the art of troublemaking in school. Not coincidentally, at the same time, my father was mastering the art of alcoholism. We were both much too successful. For my father it paved the way for his discovery of Alcoholics Anonymous, better known as AA. My entire family attended the meetings; my mother to Alanon and the kids to Alateen. This was often quite a production since there were nine children to load into the car each week. For a time, the meetings seemed to bring our family closer together, but AA lacked the staying power we were seeking. Somehow, at least in my father's case, it always seemed to give the alcoholic an out.

Still, it was thanks to AA that my father finally experienced a shift in his awareness. At one of the meetings, an announcement was made about a relaxation seminar being offered locally. Learning to relax was right up Dad's alley, especially since he couldn't recall a time in his life when he was able to truly relax. The relaxation seminar ultimately paved my father's way into his research of just what his mind could do for him. He finally understood that he had the ability, with the use of his mind, to deal with everyday stress, which somehow curbed his appetite for alcohol.

His research later led him to Silva Mind Control (now known as The Silva Method). His addiction was transformed; he now had a thirst for knowledge that evolved into his desire to share what he was learning with others. He became a Silva Instructor and soon advanced to training others.

One of the nice things about having a Silva Mind Control instructor for a father is that my eight siblings and I became his guinea pigs. We were all soon learning the unlimited potential in putting our fantastic young minds to use. Each of us found different and very individual ways to benefit from each new discovery.

As it must be when knowledge exceeds an occupation, my father became very restless in his job at the local factory. He decided it was time to find an appropriate career. He was quick in ending his ties with the company that had employed him for over fifteen years. His interest turned to the field of hypnosis. What better way to access the part of the mind where all change needs to start? With Dr. Paul Adams, author of The New Self Hypnosis, my father studied, and quickly learned, the techniques of hypnosis. He instantly recognized the processes of The Silva Method; they were nearly identical to the patterns of hypnosis.

As I came of age and my interest in hypnosis grew, I found myself frequenting my father's library to quench my own thirst for more information. Without conscious awareness, I decided to become a hypnotist myself. During my college years, I joined my father's practice in the small Michigan town that had been my life. After nearly five years, we decided to make the move to the larger metropolis of Phoenix, Arizona. With the help of Dr. Adams, we started our first Positive Changes Hypnosis Center®.

Phoenix offered my father and me an abundance of new information in the field of hypnosis. Within a few months of our arrival, we attended our first seminar on Neuro-Linguistic Programming (NLP). This seminar, and the training that followed, changed the course of our practice forever. We left the introductory lecture feeling elated. It was during this seminar that we were able to confirm what we had begun to suspect – that creating permanent behavior change takes much more than simply putting someone into a hypnotic trance (the main thrust of most standard hypnosis techniques). Much, much more important is having the skills to present the new information so the bio-computer (brain) can truly assimilate it and then feed it back during day-to-day activities as an effective and permanent behavior modification.

Fortunately, I was trained by some of the best NLP instructors in the country. From them I continually heard talk of a hypnotist by the name of Milton Erickson. Although Dr. Erickson is no longer with us, luck was with me in that the Erickson Institute happened to be located just a few miles from my home in Phoenix. I had a never-ending supply of information on Dr. Erickson and his therapeutic techniques. All of my clients were now the recipients for everything I was learning.

I was, and still am, fortunate enough to be a part of one of the most successful hypnosis practices in the country, with offices in the United States and Canada all using the techniques we have developed. It didn't take us long to recognize which patterns of change are truly applicable and which are only effective for impressing seminar participants.

I eventually relocated my business to Virginia Beach, Virginia, where I found a receptive community in search of ways to better their lives. Before leaving Arizona, I was asked to write a program for the Arizona Health Council to re-educate D.U.I. offenders. In so doing, I seized the opportunity to put my thoughts, techniques and patterns on paper. Thus, the patterns of Psycho-Linguistics were born. Now the patterns of Psycho-Linguistics are used in centers across North America, through the Positive Changes Hypnosis Centers franchise chain. You can contact one in your area by going online to www.positivechanges.com.

It would be virtually impossible to give credit to all of the authors, educators, and trainers who contributed to the development of these techniques. One thing you can depend upon, however, is that these methods will continually be modified and enhanced as new client needs are presented to the Positive Changes franchisees and me.

The Psycho-Linguistics patterns are not intended to diminish hypnosis, NLP, positive thinking, meditation, mind control, creative visualization or any other mind technology. Rather, it is to share what I have found successful for my clients and me. There is no superior change technology; I have found profound benefits in each method. We are fortunate to be living in the information age, where there are abundant resources available for self-help or for helping others to make changes or improvements to their day-to-day lives. Enter the realm of Psycho-Linguistics with these two thoughts in mind: "The law of mind is the law of belief," and, "There are no limits to consciousness."

The First Step is to be a Master of Communication

"Communication" has been a buzzword in psychology and counseling for several years. How many couples report to marriage counselors, "We just don't communicate anymore"? But how many of these couples have ever been taught *how* to communicate? For many, it never occurred to them that they could learn how to access each other's bio-computer and speak the language of the other person's mind. They just assumed there was something wrong between them.

In order to have an impact in self-improvement or in helping others, you must first be a master of communication. You will need to know how to access the other person's *(and your own)* bio-computer.

INITIATION
What is Psycho-Linguistics?

Psycho-Linguistics *is a series of patterns* designed around strategies rather than problems. Therapists using most standard techniques will find it necessary to re-create the sensitive information surrounding the experience and then confront the patient on a conscious level, usually reproducing all of the pain and suffering as well. Also, the mechanics of most therapies infer that in some way the problem could have been avoided. The "Big Book" of Alcoholics Anonymous[1], however, points out that knowledge does not a sure cure make. On every pack of cigarettes the Surgeon General warns that cigarette smoking is hazardous to your health. Yet millions of people, even with the knowledge that each inhalation is destroying their body, will continue to practice the habit without skipping a beat. *Why?* This question is what first inspired me to look into alternative theories using a more solution-driven approach *(how to become a non-smoker)* rather than a problem-driven approach *(why you are a smoker)*.

I wanted to understand what could possibly motivate such curious behavior. This was the answer I was seeking when I started my research. What I discovered during that search is what subsequently inspired the Psycho-Linguistics *patterns,* which I outline herein.

Psycho-Linguistics bases its results on the reality that we all learn behaviors through life experience and we structure that truth as memories, which are stored through the sensory channels. Through the *Psycho-Linguistic* process, I will demonstrate how people are able to change their thinking processes and in turn change their lives. The findings are based on the hands-on results gathered through research at our franchised Positive Changes Hypnosis Centers® throughout North America.

---

[1] Alcoholics Anonymous World Services, Inc., 3rd Edition, 1976

By reviewing the origins of Psycho-Linguistics, with an emphasis on just how the patterns were developed, you will begin to get the feel for *what* Psycho-Linguistics is, and hopefully for what deeper meaning it will have in your search for a *positive change*.

In simplest terms: Psycho-Linguistics is a usable, rapid and efficient method for accessing your mind or another individual's mind and making changes to behaviors, attitudes and/or thought patterns. Psycho-Linguistics is a combined study and theory of the processes of Neuro-Linguistic Programming (NLP), hypnosis, self-talk, creative visualization, imagery, accelerated learning and Ericksonian Hypnosis. It is through the use of all of the above methods that I developed *Psycho-Linguistics: The Language of the Mind*.

The results achieved with this technology are based on the impact made to the individual's thinking process rather than on gaining a greater insight into the person's problems. This is not to suggest that modern psychology does not deal with this issue, it is simply handled in a different way.

If one's goal is to impact a person's mind, there is much more involved than simply accessing an altered state, or even saying the right words – one must say it in the right order and in a format acceptable to that individual's mind. To influence the mind, one must communicate in a language with which it can relate. The patterns of Psycho-Linguistics are designed to accelerate the process and to make the change permanent.

Through extensive research, with real people expressing real *problems*, I have come to the conclusion that the *problem* has no relevancy to the *solution*. This can be likened to physical illness in that the symptom is not the disease. If medical doctors treated only symptoms, their cure rate would be next to nil.

Understand that each person's mind is goal-striving and will do its best with whatever information is at hand. In other words, each individual simply needs to discover the unconscious triggers or previous programming involved, and make the appropriate adjustments. When done correctly, the modification allows for a free flow of communication through all channels so a new and more appropriate choice can be made.

Our minds are designed to create what we are mentally rehearsing. Unfortunately, this is not always what was wanted or intended. If one's other-than-conscious mind is convinced that one is a failure, and has been rehearsing failure through mental movies and continuous re-runs, then one will become successful at failure. On the other hand, should one rehearse success while in an altered state of awareness – not just positive affirmation but a full sensory experience – then one will experience success, because at that level of thinking the mental rehearsal and the physical action will be stored in equal measure. Through physical and mental rehearsal it will soon come to pass as reality.

One of my main purposes in developing these non-contextual techniques was for use by trainers who want to offer group processing. With Psycho-Linguistics, the individual participants are able to audit themselves and make the appropriate changes using the step-by-step procedures. Once learned, the results can be tested and adjustments can be made on a day-to-day basis. This concept follows the theory of Alcoholics Anonymous – *"One day at a time."*

"The greatest discovery of my generation is that a human being can alter his life by altering his attitudes of mind."

WILLIAM JAMES (1842-1910)

"Education is not merely a means
for earning a living
or an instrument for the acquisition of wealth.
It is... a training of the human soul
in the pursuit of truth
and the practice of virtue."

VIJAYA LAKSHMI PANDIT
President of the All-India Women's Conference
from 1941 to 1943
and Founder and President of
All-India Save the Children

Chapter One

History of **Behavior-Change** Technology

How does one approach the world with techniques so divergent from mainstream awareness? Well, the truth of the matter is that hypnosis, Neuro-Linguistic Programming, creative visualization, imagery and self-talk are not really so far removed from more traditional modes of therapy – they are simply modified for delivery through altered states of consciousness and in a non-contextual format.

Definitions for each of the above modalities follow the same presuppositions as you find in this writing and support the premise that if one person can master a skill or behavior, then it is possible to model that person and train another to master the same skill or behavior.

I have spent quite some time now deliberating over how to present a clear dictionary-style definition of hypnosis. I have come to the conclusion that hypnosis is likely only definable through experience. Once defined, one might say it is very similar to the explication of visualization because, in most cases, while using imagery, the person is in a state of hypnosis without realizing it. Andre M. Weitzenhoffer describes hypnosis as, *"a condition or state of selective hyper suggestibility brought about in an individual (subject) through the use of certain specific psychological or physical manipulations of this individual by another person (hypnotist)."* He goes on to state that, *"...self-hypnosis is equivalent to a two-person interaction in which part of the self appears to take over the role of hypnotist..."*[2] Therefore, the above definition would apply to self-hypnosis as well.

Although somewhat vaguer than Weitzenhoffer's, my definition is as follows:

Hypnosis is a selected state of consciousness that one enters into for a specific purpose.

Less than vague, you might say? Precisely my point. Hypnosis can be used for anything and everything relating to the mind. Although best known for habit and behavior changes, hypnosis has proven to be highly effective for life enhancement, study skills, pain management, self-motivation, relaxation and even increased intuition. It has improved and often saved marriages and is extremely effective for sexual dysfunction. The list is endless. The front cover of the Positive Changes Hypnosis Centers' information booklet says it best: *"All Positive Change Starts in the Mind."*[3] Can you think of a truer statement?

WHAT IS THE HISTORY OF HYPNOSIS?

Although I believe hypnosis and imagery have been around since the dawn of man, typically without conscious knowledge of what was at play, I will start with what little is known of its practice through history.

About 4000 years ago in the temples of Egypt, the high priests and initiates used forms of imagery and hypnosis to train the more affluent officials to overcome physical pain. These healing sanctuaries, known to the Egyptians as Sleep Temples or Dream Temples, were used for healing of both physical and psychological problems. A more mystical form of hypnosis was used for forecasting future events.

---

[2] Weitzenhoffer, Andre M., General Techniques of Hypnotism, 1957, Grune & Stratton, Inc. pg. 32

[3] Positive Changes, Inc. Copyright 1990

In another part of the world, ancient Greece, "sleeping rooms" were used by the priests of the time and served the same function that a hypnotist performs in modern times. They would relax the person, usually a high official, and guide him through the past or into the future. The sleeping rooms were often used for visionary strategic planning and for contact with the gods.

Archeological excavations show evidence of sleeping temples in ancient Rome and even Great Britain. The ruins of a sleeping temple can be viewed today at an archeological site in Lydney Park, Gloucestershire, United Kingdom.

Hypnosis has been given many different names over the centuries. Whether it was known as mesmerism, meditation, or hypnosis, the basis of its use was to go to a specific state of consciousness for a purpose. Hypnosis and imagery methods didn't start gaining any real notice until a flamboyant Austrian physician, Franz Anton Mesmer, started his own brand of hypnotism during the late 18th century. His colorful ways brought attention to this unseen power that is within each and every one of us. The term *"mesmerized"* was coined after his methods became widely known.

Mesmer was flashy and mystical in his work. Using his eyes, the spoken word and a series of waves of the hands and arms, he built an incredible intensity between himself and the subject. Although he didn't understand what was at play, the end result was often astonishing.

Mesmer asserted that the human body contained a certain fluid that accounted for the phenomena of magnetism and that this effect could emanate from the eyes and the hands of the *"magnetist"* (himself). We know today that the effect was actually produced by something very different. He had only a small piece of the puzzle, but it did lay the foundation for what is known today as hypnosis, visualization and imagery.

It was Dr. James Braid (1795-1860) who coined the term hypnosis, naming it after the Greek word *hupnos,* meaning *sleep.* Virtually since the inception of the word, *hypnosis* has been the most widely misunderstood term in history. Even an 1847 decree by the Roman Catholic Church could not dissipate the many misconceptions surrounding hypnosis. The Church's decree stated in part, "Having removed all misconceptions...the use of hypnosis is indeed merely an act of making use of physical media, and is not morally forbidden, provided that it does not tend towards an illicit end." Braid pioneered the induction of hypnosis through eye fixation. His primary technique was to ask the subject to focus on a bright object held close to the eyes. Continual staring at the bright, shining object would fatigue the eyes, causing the lids to get heavy and close. These techniques ultimately led to the popular images of the hypnotist holding a swinging watch as seen in movies and on television.

In the state of hypnosis most people, even in the deepest trance, will remember what was said and experienced throughout the session. Only a small cross section of the population will awaken with amnesia after a session of hypnosis. Many people cannot tell the difference between a hypnotized state and a *"waking"* state, and will insist hypnosis did not occur when it most definitely did.

During a stage hypnosis performance, for example, a young woman may be asked whether she believes she is hypnotized and will respond with an emphatic, "No!" The hypnotist need only say the word "sleep" and she will immediately fall like a limp dishrag into a deep state. Upon awakening the same young woman will insist that she is not hypnotized, but will fall into an immediate hypnotic sleep with the suggestion to do so.

Fortunately, the twenty-first century medical community is awakening to the promise hypnosis holds for aiding patients pre and post surgery and for overcoming chronic pain, even when drugs fail.

It is not the intention of this book to give you a historical breakdown on hypnosis, but to give you real proof that the client's knowledge that hypnosis occurred is not necessary for the change to be made. The purpose of this book is to give you a fresh look at what I have termed Psycho-Linguistics, *"The Language of the Mind."* However, like all types of mind training, there is a part to be played by the subject.

Although hypnosis and imagery in one fashion or another have existed for millennia, some people still question its validity. For the tens of thousands of people who have benefited from hypnosis, the debate over its validity means little.

Mind technology, such as hypnosis, imagery and self-talk, is gaining more of a scientific base all the time. In fact, with today's new technology, such as Neuro-Linguistic Programming, almost anyone can successfully help people as long as one's heart and intentions are in the right place.

Also, the modern hypnotist will use scientific equipment such as advanced bio-feed-in machines, which utilize light and sound technology. The Positive Changes Hypnosis Centers light and sound machine (see Chapter 17), takes care of placing the client into the receptive state needed for acceptance of new information. In today's world, people are realizing that the only thing limiting them is their own willingness to believe.

It is true in many respects that hypnosis is a conviction phenomenon. The client must be convinced that the hypnotic process will make a difference. Instilling this confidence is one of the most important jobs a hypnotist can perform. It is essential that the subject believe in a power greater than his or her own conscious mind for help and support. Once this belief system is instilled, the hypnotist's job is well on its way. From here, the other-than-conscious mind can enter into the process and guide the client's thinking in the direction of the desired result.

When people become addicted, whether it is to drugs, food, alcohol or tobacco, they are, without exception, seeking a positive feeling. Therefore, all addictions have underlying positive intentions. Doug Rushkoff and Patrick Wells tell us that, *"Getting high is one of the most natural of human urges."*[4] All humans have a need for periods of non-ordinary consciousness. Because of this, it appears to be a biological urge. Of course in recent decades *"getting high"* is considered at worst illegal and at best irresponsible.

Through the use of Psycho-Linguistics, clients are taught that their positive intention, or high, is not only *"okay,"* it is necessary and natural. The individual is then guided to fill in the pieces for achieving a high without the need for drugs or addictions. They can transform their addictive behavior into something positive and productive.

It is a fact that everyone alive already knows how to get high naturally. As infants, we were all open channels for receiving signals through all five senses. Because of this, the newborn has no information upon

---

[4] Rushkoff, Douglas and Wells, Patrick, Free Rides – How to Get High Without Drugs, 1991, Bantam Doubleday, Dell Publishing, New York, New York

which to judge the information received, everything is experienced and nothing is filtered. However, as the child grows into adulthood, he or she must put on filters as the ability to focus, concentrate and learn becomes necessary. Soon, the total aliveness of full-sensory experience is lost, but the memory of complete awareness remains.

Psycho-Linguistics is designed to darken, quiet and desensitize the remembrances of the less-than-positive experiences of the past and to re-awaken the memories of the natural joy found in living "*high.*"

"Because we do not understand the brain very well we are constantly tempted to use the latest technology as a model for trying to understand it. In my childhood we were always assured that the brain was a telephone switchboard. ['What else could it be?'] I was amused to see that Sherrington, the great British neuroscientist, thought that the brain worked like a telegraph system. Freud often compared the brain to hydraulic and electro-magnetic systems. Leibniz compared it to a mill, and I am told some of the ancient Greeks thought the brain functions like a catapult. At present, obviously, the metaphor is the digital computer."

JOHN R. SEARLE, *Minds, Brains and Science,* **p 44**

Chapter Two

What is *Hypnosis* and *Imagery?*

Over the years I have encountered strong evidence that there are innumerable misconceptions surrounding the science of hypnosis, even in the scientific and medical communities. Perhaps this relates to the origins of hypnosis, which were steeped in superstition and mysticism.

A large percentage of the general public believes that a hypnotist holds some kind of mystical power over the subject, and it would appear that way if you were watching a hypnotist perform a stage show.

One cannot influence people to do something against their moral code or that they would not do with any other persuasion method. The people who "perform" in a stage show must have agreed on some level to do what the hypnotist requests. If people choose not to be hypnotized, there is no hypnotist who can force them to do so against their will.

Many of the hypnosis processes outlined in this book are loosely based on *Ericksonian Hypnosis,* named after the renowned psychiatrist and hypnotist, Dr. Milton Erickson. His processes involved creating a relaxed mind to aid in the treatment of mental disorders. Unlike the stage hypnotist, who takes away conscious control, through the Ericksonian model, control is given to the subject.

Hypnosis in this context is not brain washing but may be more appropriately termed *brain cleansing*. When an individual comes to a trained hypnotist, he or she is usually in a state of loss. For example, a woman who has smoked cigarettes for 35 years, and is now in poor health, probably believes she lacks willpower, and is convinced she can't quit smoking on her own. In other words, she has hypnotized herself into believing that she can't change on her own. The hypnotist's job is to *cleanse* her mind of such a limited thought and direct her back to the power within her.

WHAT IS THE CONSCIOUS MIND?

The conscious mind accounts for approximately 8% of the mind's total thinking and processing power. The conscious mind is the part of you aware at this moment – it is the part of you now reading and comprehending this book. The conscious mind is subject to time. It is analytical, logical, and stores our active memories. We perform activities such as balancing our checkbook, conversing with a co-worker, or writing a letter with our conscious mind.

While our conscious mind is what makes us *aware* of who we are, the other 92% of our mind stores the *reality* of who we are.

WHAT IS THE OTHER-THAN-CONSCIOUS MIND?

The analogy of the computer comes in handy once again when describing the mind's capacity. The *other-than-conscious* portion of the mind stores data from every thought and experience you ever had. It contains your values, your core beliefs, your self-image and your internal map of the world.

The other-than-conscious mind works automatically, without conscious effort. Physical functions such as your heartbeat, breathing, digestion, and regeneration of bones and tissues are all performed at the other-than-conscious level.

The other-than-conscious mind houses our creativity, emotions and imagination. Therefore, time does not exist here. We can bring a past memory into the present moment and fantasize a future all at the same time. We can be fat or slim, sick or healthy, rich or poor, unhappy or happy. In other words, there are no limits at the other-than-conscious level. Is it any wonder hypnotists prefer to work in this realm?

WHAT IS THE CRITICAL FACTOR?

Our minds have mechanisms that protect our beliefs, values and us. One such mechanism is the *critical factor*. It acts as the gatekeeper between the conscious and other-than-conscious. The critical factor's sole purpose is to either allow or prevent suggestions from entering the other-than-conscious mind.

The critical factor has good intentions. Unfortunately, change is considered a threat to our nervous system. Therefore, the critical factor tends to throw out suggestions that don't match our existing programming – even good suggestions.

In order to make a permanent change, the programming must reach the other-than-conscious mind, and the only way to get to there is by bypassing the critical factor.

Spaced repetition is the mind's natural way of circumventing the critical factor. As an example, repeating a certain behavior through willpower eventually develops into an existing program, thus breaking through the critical factor.

The much easier way to get around the critical factor is hypnosis. The guided relaxation, willingness of the subject, enhanced imaginative abilities and spaced repetition of the new behavior all conspire to subdue the critical factor and fully impact the other-than-conscious mind.

WHAT IS THE ROLE OF THE OTHER-THAN-CONSCIOUS MIND IN HYPNOSIS?

Let us take a moment to think of how we came to be who we are right now. Our belief structure, whether valid or not, is what molded us. Throughout our lives, other people will shape our future unless we take back our power. This is the power of choice. Hypnosis is by far the best modality for reaching that place where the belief structure was formed and where it can be changed. I am referring to the *other-than-conscious* mind.

There are five components necessary for an effective hypnotic induction that reaches the other-than-conscious mind and makes permanent changes. They are:

1. *Motivation*
2. *Relaxation*
3. *Imagination*
4. *Suggestion*
5. *Spaced Repetition*

The other-than-conscious mind has no power to reason. Therefore, it accepts and acts upon any fact or suggestion. When all five of the above components are in place, the critical factor is subdued, and positive suggestions are easily delivered to the other-than-conscious mind, where they become desirable new behaviors.

A person in a state of hypnosis will not do anything he or she would not agree to do otherwise. Also, contrary to what you may have seen in the movies, a person is fully capable of telling lies while under hypnosis. Naturally, hypnosis works best when there is a conscious desire on the part of the subject to make a change. Once this conscious agreement is obtained, a well-trained hypnotist will have the ability to access the client's bio-computer *(brain)* and feed in the appropriate suggestions.

I believe it is our natural and divine right to have what we want in our lives. One of my favorite excerpts from the Bible reads, "If you abide in me, and my words abide in you, ask whatever you wish, and it will be done for you."[5] There are no limitations within this statement. Thus, it applies in every area of your life.

[5] John 15:7 NASB

Another common misconception about hypnosis is that only weak-minded people can be hypnotized. This is totally false and, in fact, the reverse is true. The higher intelligence level of the client, the better hypnosis, imagery or any other change technology will work. After all, hypnosis is a tool. People don't really change because of hypnosis, but they do make changes while in a state of hypnosis. There is a subtle difference. In the state of hypnosis, you are experiencing an expanded state of consciousness or awareness. It is a state where solutions are stored as possibilities. Here is where the hypnotist's role becomes vital. The job of the hypnotist is to help the subject access these solutions and apply them in his or her own life. All hypnosis is self-hypnosis – without the willingness of the subject, the hypnotist's job is certain to fail.

HOW DOES IT FEEL TO BE HYPNOTIZED?

Most people move in and out of light trance states all day long. They daydream, remember, imagine, dwell on the past, dream of the future, replay conversations, carry on internal dialogue and more. Is it any surprise that most people come out of a controlled hypnosis process declaring they didn't "feel hypnotized"? They don't "feel" it, because it is a natural and familiar state.

Most people remain consciously aware of their surroundings while in hypnosis. Many will experience one or more of the following sensations. Inform you clients that any of these sensations are possible so they do not get caught off guard. The first time my wife was hypnotized, she was so alarmed by a sense of energy moving through her body, it shocked her right out of the trance. When a client reports feeling one of these sensations, be sure to reinforce that it is normal and a good sign that hypnosis is, in fact, taking place.

WHAT SENSATIONS ARE ASSOCIATED WITH HYPNOSIS?

- *Tingling in fingertips, toes or limbs*
- *A sense of lightness*
- *A floating sensation*
- *A sense of heaviness*
- *A feeling of sinking into the chair*
- *A sense of energy moving throughout the body*
- *Rapid eyelid fluttering*
- *An increase or decrease in salivation*
- *A feeling of no-feeling (as if one's body has melted away)*

Most people believe that hypnosis is something one either can or cannot do. I've encountered hundreds of misguided individual who comment, "I don't think I can be hypnotized." With an understanding smile I explain that being hypnotized is something anyone can learn, and that the results are cumulative. The more the techniques are practiced, the better hypnotic subject one becomes.

With the techniques outlined in this book, you will know how to guide yourself or others through the hypnotic process – from the first meeting, through the gathering of necessary information, to the layout of a successful plan of action and client follow up. Before you ever begin, however, there are a few steps that must be taken. The key to success in the hypnosis field is to be armed with a toolbox full of useful techniques and processes. First and foremost, you must be able to put yourself into the hypnotic state so you can relate with your clients' experiences.

THE TEN STEPS TO SELF-HYPNOSIS

In its true sense, all hypnosis is self-hypnosis. Only the person going into the hypnotic state, for whatever purpose, has the ability to make a change happen. Whether the participants are using these techniques or another, the hypnotic state is simply the method of access to the place within the mind where the new and more appropriate choices are created.

There are numerous ways to put oneself into the altered state of hypnosis. From there it is up to each individual. Whether one is going into trance using a key word such as *"aum,"* or by rolling the eyes up to a ten o'clock position, one is practicing the art and science of hypnosis. Over the years it has been called many things; mind control, transcendental meditation (TM), or creative visualization. All of these altered states fall under the definition of hypnosis. *(Definition: Hypnosis is a selected state of consciousness that one enters for a specific purpose.)*

This first technique of hypnosis is what I would consider one of the easiest and quickest for anyone to master. It is important to point out that deep altered states are not necessary for profound change to occur, but it does help the body to release some of the unconscious stress of the day, thereby freeing up the energy of the mind to work on the specific solution at hand. The easiest way to use this outline is to read the steps into a tape recorder, leaving a long pause between steps, and then play it back one or two times a day or until the process is learned without the script.

There is a stage performer, "The Amazing Kreskin," who says he is willing to pay $100,000 to anyone who can prove that the hypnotic state exists. His claim is that there is no such state as hypnosis, only the *"power of suggestion."* He uses this exact same self-hypnosis technique in his seminars, although he swears it is not hypnosis.

I believe Kreskin's shenanigans simply prove the general public's overall ignorance about hypnosis and their unfortunate gullibility when it comes to tricks of semantics by publicity-seeking entertainers.

1. Get into a comfortable position.

You will soon discover that relaxation is a key element to the hypnotic state. Place yourself in a comfortable chair or lay down. Choose another location besides your bed since this is your place of sleep. For this procedure to be effective you will want to remain completely aware. Place your hands comfortably by your side or in your lap. From this moment on, concentrate on your breathing. Begin to connect the breath as you breathe in and out. In time this will come naturally to you and conscious effort will no longer be necessary. Breathe in a full breath and at the end transition directly to releasing a full breath and then repeat the process. Imagine you are breathing in a circle. There is no end and no beginning to your breathing. This process of connected breathing alone can place you into an altered state of consciousness.

2. Close your eyes and repeat three times to yourself the amount of time you wish to remain in the hypnotized state.

In the state of self-hypnosis there is no time, or more precisely, while in a deep state you are unaware of time. There is a scientific explanation for this phenomenon. Without getting too complicated, let me explain. We all operate within four basic brainwave patterns. They are known as Beta, which is wide awake; Alpha, which is a relaxed state and has also been found through research to be a powerful learning state; Theta, also a very relaxed state and a place for super learning; and; Delta, associated with deep sleep. Hypnosis, and a state of super-learning, takes place within the brainwave states of Alpha and Theta. While a subject is in these states, there appears to be a sense of time distortion; one minute could feel like an hour. Time does not seem to exist or have any impact on the subject and access to a greater reality is then granted. In actuality, that reality is your full imagination, which is the true tool of hypnosis or any change technology.

Also, the state may feel so good to you that without giving yourself the suggestion to return within a particular time frame, you could find yourself staying in the self-hypnotic state for hours at a time. Although this is not a problem, it is not necessary. Hypnosis is known for fast and effective change and there really isn't any reason to stay in hypnosis for more than 20 to 30 minutes at a time.

3. Imagine a blackboard and place the number 25 on it. Envision yourself erasing that number and replace it with the number 24... then 23... 22... Each number is guiding you deeper than the number before. Continue this process until you reach zero.

This process is to give your conscious mind something to do while your other-than-conscious mind relaxes your body.

4. Become aware of your body and scan it for the level of relaxation achieved. Imagine that you are filling your body up with a solution that will protect you and keep you from harm.

The purpose of this is to narrow your attention down to the different parts of your body and give you the feeling of being in a safe place. It is from this safe place that your other-than-conscious mind will successfully help you through the changes.

5. Imagine that you are creating your ideal place of relaxation.

Create a place where you can be comfortable and at peace. This ideal place of relaxation could be anywhere. Whether on a sandy beach with the ocean waves lapping at your feet, or atop a mountain with a clean, brisk breeze ruffling your hair and cooling your cheeks, it is your creation. There are no limits here. So that inventing it will be enjoyable every time, you can make enhancements each time you go to your ideal place.

6. Go now to that personal place of relaxation and imagine yourself drifting off into a dream and in the dream all that you want, all that you need and all that you desire has come true. (Remember, in dreams all things are possible and there are no limitations to consciousness.)

This step is important in the process of self-imagery because dreams are a surefire way of making contact with the other-than-conscious mind, which is the part of you that will create successful changes in the future.

7. Step into your dream. Begin to see what you would be seeing, hear what you would be hearing and feel what you would be feeling. Act as if everything is actually happening all around you.

Every night during our dreams we are given suggestions by the other-than-conscious mind. Yet we often ignore our nighttime counsel, discounting the information as "just a dream." But remember that your mind is a servomechanism – a goal-striving, success-oriented, bio-chemical machine that doesn't know how to fail. However, problems arise if we have fed in failure information. The bio-computer cannot help but feed the same failure information back. When this happens it is time to make a change, which is what imagery is all about. Everyone is working perfectly. People are not wrong or broken; they have just been misinformed. They tend to believe that if they continue to think and act in the same way that somehow, some way, a different outcome is just around the corner. But, as the saying goes, if you continue to think what you have always thought, you will continue to get what you have always got! So be brave and live your dreams.

8. **Move yourself into the future to the date and time when you are convinced that you deserve and have what you want, need and desire.**
   (You are creating a vacuum for your mind where it can place your wishes into sequence.)

The relevance of this step is two-fold. First, hypnosis is a conviction phenomenon in more ways than one. You must be convinced that you can and will have your wants, needs and desires fulfilled. Secondly, in order for hypnosis to work you must place into sequence the successful steps that your bio-computer will need to follow.[6]

9. **Starting from that future date and moving backwards in time, make a review in your mind of all that you will do and all that you will experience to bring about the fulfillment of your desires.**

The purpose of this step is to give your bio-computer an alternate view of the future by storing it as if the success has already occurred.

---

[6] Ask, and it shall be given to you; seek, and you shall find; knock, and it shall be opened to you. Matthew 7:7 NASB

10. **Count from one to five, until you are back to fully awakened consciousness. (Give yourself the following suggestion.)** *"I'm going to count from one to five and at the count of five I will be wide awake, feeling fine and in perfect health. One... Two... Three... All changes and modifications are being made from my other-than-conscious to my conscious mind... Four... and, Five... wide awake."* **Take three full breaths realizing with each breath that all you have experienced is now truth for you... and this is so.**

Understand that you are bringing yourself from a state near sleep to fully awake in a matter of seconds. Some people seem to maintain the incorrect belief that one can be stuck in hypnosis forever. This is totally false. It is impossible for someone to remain in a hypnotic state permanently and this has never happened. You would simply fall into a natural sleep and awaken after a short nap.

WHO CAN BE HYPNOTIZED?

Generally speaking, every normal person is hypnotizable – that is, people with an IQ of at least 70 who have no severe mental disorders. In my opinion, the right hypnotist can help even those with IQs below 70. Throughout my eighteen years of practicing mind technology, I have witnessed many fantastic transformations in a variety of people from all walks of life, proving time and again that there are truly no limits to consciousness or the mind's ability to make behavior changes and enhancements.

The following techniques are designed to help the hypnotist choose those subjects who have the ability to reach a deep hypnotic state. Keep in mind that deep trance states are not a prerequisite to change, but rather a resource.

The following tests are given to help in assessing what percentage will accept *direct suggestions* and what percentage will need *inferred suggestions*. Some people will, by nature, accept what you are saying and go along with all that you ask of them (direct). Others will assume or infer that they know what you "mean" for them to do (inferred). In later chapters the concept of direct versus inferred is explained in detail.

"Success is not the result of spontaneous combustion. You must set yourself on fire."

Reggie Leach

WHAT ARE PSYCHO-LINGUISTICS TESTING PROCESSES?

For simplicity in writing, this portion will assume that we are testing a female client, although the testing techniques will work with equal effect for women and men alike.

A. FINGER MAGNETS.

Have the subject place her hands together separating the two index fingers. Ask her to look down at her fingers and imagine that at the fingertips there are two magnets and they are being drawn together. Once the fingers touch together give strong suggestions that she will not be able to take them apart. In fact, the harder she tries the more difficult it will become. Once these suggestions are given, ask her to *"try to take them apart."* Watch her attempts and when she has failed a few times give her the suggestion that at the count of three her fingers will easily come apart.

Figure 1. Finger Magnets Step 1

Figure 2. Finger Magnets Step 2

Don't be too concerned with whether the subject is able to take her fingers apart. Rather, look for her ability to accept a direct suggestion. The purpose of the test is to find those subjects who can create what is known as selective thinking and also to screen those subjects who test as inferred suggestible. In truth, you are testing your subject's imagination and ability to take a direct suggestion.

Some people will become concerned when they suspect they have failed a test. They begin to fear that they are not hypnotizable. It is virtually impossible to fail the test. Under no circumstances do you tell your clients that they have failed a test. Simply explain that they are going through a testing process, one which they cannot fail. These tests are for you, the hypnotist, to gather information you will use later during the altered state.

As you gain experience with these tests, you will begin to recognize a strong correlation between "right brain thinkers" and direct suggestibility and "left brain thinkers" and inferred suggestibility. This result is logical since the right hemisphere controls creativity and the left hemisphere controls precise thinking. In reality, the test result is of little importance to the subject but is of immeasurable value to a trained hypnotist who will use the information later during the altered state.

When testing subjects who are inferred, it is very important that you point out to them that hypnosis or change cannot occur without their consent. I let them know they are being tested on their imagination, not intelligence. It is essential for an inferred subject to know that there is no failure, only feedback. So keep your perceptual filters open for any clues that your subject might display. The above statement is true for all testing processes.

"What we have to do is to be forever curiously testing new opinions and courting new impressions."

WALTER PATER
English critic (1839-1894)

B. HAND CLASP.

Figure 3. Hand Clasp

Place the subject's hands straight out in front of her in a clasp and have her imagine that, as she squeezes down, a vise is pressing against the outside of the hands making it impossible for her to separate them. Give the suggestion that as she tries to take her hands apart it will become more and more difficult. Then, ask her to *"just try to take them apart."* Watch the hands closely. Then tell her that at the count of three the vise will be released and her hands will be free. Count her out by counting from one to three to ensure a return to full awareness.

C. BALLOON & BOOK.

The subject places her hands straight out in front of her body. Have her imagine that a balloon has been tied to the wrist of one hand. Ask her to turn the other hand over and imagine that a heavy book has been placed in it and as the book is getting heavier and heavier the other hand is becoming lighter and lighter, as if the balloon is lifting it into the air. Ask her to close her eyes and use her imagination. When there is a distance between the two hands, have her open her eyes and look at the placement of her hands. If your subject's hands did not move, which will be the case if the subject is inferred, simply ask that she return her hands to her lap only

Figure 4. Balloon & Book Step 1

Figure 5. Balloon & Book Step 2

as slowly as she can recognize the difference between the two. When her hands return to her lap, ask her to open her eyes once again.

D. EYE ROLL TEST.

Place your finger on the subject's forehead at the hairline and ask her to keep her eyes open and roll them upward as if looking through the top of her head at the place where your finger is touching. Give her the suggestion that with her eyes rolled upward to slowly close the eyelids down.

Figure 6. Eye Roll Test

Pay attention to the amount of white of the eye that is showing as the eyelids roll down. If there is a good portion of white showing and only a small amount of the iris visible, chances are the person is a deep subject. No one quite knows what the connection is or why this phenomenon occurs, but it has proven true time and again.

E. EYE CLOSURE.

This technique can be used immediately following the Eye Roll Test or alone. Ask the subject to close her eyes and imagine that the eyelids are so loose, so limp, and so relaxed that she won't be able to open them. (*Compound the suggestion*). When you feel that she is relaxed, suggest, "*Just try to open them.*" Watch closely as she tries and when she has failed a few times, give her the suggestion that at the count of three her eyes will open and she will once again be wide awake. Count her back up from one to three.

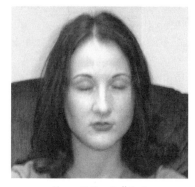

Figure 7. Eye Roll Test

Figure 8. Hypnotic Stare

F. HYPNOTIC STARE.

The Hypnotic Stare is the process most commonly associated with stage hypnosis and should be used with extreme caution. I use this test only with those subjects who have previously tested as deep subjects.

Ask the subject to look into your eyes and not to look away. (*You will continually gaze directly at the point between the eyes at the bridge of her nose, and not look away.*) Place your hands at the sides of the subject's head a few inches away to block peripheral vision. Give the suggestion: "*You are going to listen to my voice and my voice only....* *Your eyelids are getting heavier and heavier but you are going to try to keep them open... heavier and heavier.*" Continue with the suggestions until the eyelids flutter and then give the command, "*Sleep!*" BE PREPARED TO CATCH THE SUBJECT.

IS THE TEST SUBJECT DIRECTLY SUGGESTIBLE OR INFERRED SUGGESTIBLE?

The purpose in these tests is two-fold. First, they let you know just how willingly the person's conscious mind will take part in the session. For one reason or another, the young woman in this example has sought out a hypnotist for assistance. Before you would be able to effectively help her make her desired changes, her modes of access and communication must be discovered. These tests let you determine how her bio-computer takes in information.

If her bio-computer takes her hands apart during the Finger Magnets or Hand Clasp technique, you know that her mind is taking suggestions in an inferred way. In other words, she is inferring your meaning. You, as the hypnotist, will need to use inferred language patterns. The best way to access an inferred subject is through *sleight-of-mouth patterns*. Also known as *imbedded commands*, sleight-of-mouth patterns are used to persuade someone to do something without specifically telling him or her what to do.

If during the Finger Magnet technique the test subject's fingers stuck together or during the Hand Clasp test the hands remained clasped tightly, then there is a strong possibility that she will respond well to direct suggestion. A subject that is directly suggestible will most likely be more responsive, or able to do suggested movements with her physical body. This in no way means that the person who doesn't pass these tests successfully is unable to use hypnosis. As long as the right patterns are used and the inferred person is allowed to place them into her own context, the results are the same. The purpose is not only to find out whether she can successfully imagine, but it also lets you know if she takes direct suggestion or if she is making inferences in her mind as to what you are suggesting or want her to do.

The same is true with the Balloon and Book technique except it allows the hypnotist to more fully access the client's imagination. If you find that her imagination process is very good, even if she failed the two tests previous to the Balloon test, you will find that she will readily accept direct suggestions.

The hypnotist's job is to cultivate the imagination. Because the imagination is such a powerful state of consciousness, it is probably the most important access. Hypnosis is the use of the mind, or the use of the imagination, to accomplish a goal.

The Eye Roll and Eye Closure tests are used every day in the Positive Changes Hypnosis Centers. These tests help the subject to create a selective state of consciousness. In that state, the person can receive a direct suggestion to follow and this is the hypnotist's opportunity to discover whether the subject is going to go along with the suggestions. From the Eye Roll and Eye Closure, the subject can be taken directly from testing into a deep state of relaxation. The deeper the individual can go into relaxation, the better she will respond upon awakening. This is because the brainwave patterns can be influenced by deep relaxation. In hypnosis you are accessing the brainwave patterns of Alpha and Theta. In a training setting you will typically be accessing in the realm of Alpha.

"True silence is the rest of the mind; it is to the body, nourishment and refreshment."

WILLIAM PENN

WHAT ARE THE KEY DIFFERENCES BETWEEN DIRECT AND INFERRED SUGGESTIBILITY?

It is unfortunate that most hypnotists are taught only a directly suggestible approach. They are trained to place someone into a trance, tell him or her exactly what to see, hear and experience and then expect everyone placed under their spell to go out and make changes exactly as directed. Stage hypnosis has proven that only one out of every ten people is truly directly suggestible. These are the people who can be told that ammonia is perfume and, while inhaling it deeply, smell a sweet and flowery scent. With these clients you are able to perform physical manifestations, such as hand levitation, to demonstrate the direct phenomena of a hypnotic state. These people are usually aware that they were in an altered state and will experience a much deeper trance than most.

On another end of the spectrum we have the inferred suggestible person or, as known by some hypnotists, the emotionally suggestible subject. It is not very likely that a standard direct suggestion will have any affect on an inferred client. However, if you imply suggestions toward a planned direction, the inferred client can create the change in his or her own way.

As an example, *"I'm not sure exactly when these changes are going to take place, but you are."* This suggestion offers an outlet for the imagination to take over and place the changes where the client wants them.

To an inferred suggestible person the following direct suggestion would probably not be effective: *"You are going to change your smoking habits for good. Upon awakening you will crush your pack of cigarettes and be a non-smoker forever."*

This is a very direct suggestion. The inferred suggestible client's mind would probably be very busy trying to figure out how and when this may or may not occur. And, if this client didn't immediately arise from the session with an urge to crush a pack of cigarettes, he or she would be quite convinced that the hypnosis did not work. To an inferred suggestible person, you would be more likely to set up success with:

"I'm not sure what happened during this time of relaxation, but you are. Something wonderful happened and upon awakening you will find the right time, and I'm not sure exactly what time that will be, but you will rid yourself completely of tobacco and nicotine without any conscious effort. You will simply walk away. It could be today upon awakening, it could be tomorrow, or in weeks to come, but at some time you will make the decision to deal with the problem once and for all – to set yourself free. That's right; it may be as early as today."

When dealing with an inferred suggestible person, it's important that he or she is always being guided in the direction of an outcome. This is where the suggestibility testing comes into play. If someone is unable to do the testing, such as when the direct suggestion is given that the eyelids and muscles are so loose, limp and relaxed that they won't open at all and then the eyes pop open, there is a pretty good chance that this person is an inferred suggestible person. What was heard in his or her mind was "You can't open your eyes," and the immediate response was "Yes, I can," and the eyes flew open. The directly suggestible person would create the response by simply imagining the eyelids heavy and relaxed. The direct person's response would be, "Okay, I can imagine that," and the eyes will remain locked into place.

Another quick and easy tip is to monitor the way in which people present information. If they infer information while communicating to others, their brain will usually take in directly suggestible comments. If they communicate directly, there is a strong probability that they will take inferred suggestions inwardly. There is a phenomenon within the brain that will cause it to give out information in the opposite manner from how it is received.

WHAT IS THE ROLE OF THE IMAGINATION?

The imagination is perhaps the most vital ingredient in the Psycho-Linguistics session, as well as in any hypnosis session. The word imagination is, in my opinion, misspelled; it should be spelled image-a-nation. A nation representing a person's map of reality (*the belief structure*), and image, meaning the way that map is perceived within the individual's mind.

If, in your imagination, you can paint a picture, and can hear the sounds and experience the feelings, then you have imaged it and now it is a nation (map of reality) in your mind. What you perceive in your mind will come to pass as reality. The bio-computer, or the brain, now has all necessary information for bringing this new reality into being through behaviors, attitudes and actions.

WHAT ARE BRAINWAVE PATTERNS?

We all have a balance of brainwaves at play during our day, whether we are active, sedentary or in deep sleep. Our brain's rhythms move from Beta to Alpha, through Theta and into Delta off and on throughout the day. It is through these brainwaves that we access the memories or sequences of thought that make up our personalities and create the differences between us. When a subject is in a relaxed and receptive state, he or she is in the best position for making a behavior change that will be permanent.

Although there are four distinctive brainwave patterns, every human brain functions with multiple brainwave activity.

1. Beta State (The Reactionary Mind).

(*20-13 cycles per second*) Beta is the state in which your conscious mind is accessed. It is the wide awake state in which you keep track of your life, such as paying your bills, setting up your appointment calendar for the day, and balancing your checkbook. It is your analytical mind. Within its realm is the part of you that is at times self-conscious and at other times controlling. This is the awakened state of consciousness and within this realm fear, frustration, anxiety and self-doubt reside. It is in this state when you "re-act" instead of interacting. This is also the state where most people try to make changes. That is why it is so important to enter into an altered state where the other-than-conscious mind can help.

2. Alpha State (The Intuitive Mind).

(13 to 7 cycles per second) When you are feeling very creative, relaxed and at ease, you are probably functioning in Alpha. This is the place where there is no time and no limitations. In Alpha your creative juices seem to flow without end and the body is in a place of serenity. If you have ever watched an artist at work, you will notice how creativity can seem to emanate from within the physical body. The artist's eyes are usually very intense, but other-worldly, and the body seems to flow as if each limb were poured from a rich fluid. If tested, the artist's brainwave pattern would surely be heavily in Alpha. Most artists, writers, composers, and poets can work for long hours, often through the night, without any awareness of the time as it ticks away on the clock and then will suddenly be amazed when realizing the amount of time that has elapsed. Alpha knows no time and holds no limitations. One easy way to reach the pleasant state of Alpha is by quietly listening to baroque music.

3. Theta State (The Inventive Mind).

(7 to 4 cycles per second) Meditation is the best known access to the Theta state of consciousness. It is a deeply relaxed state on the brink of sleep. With the help of certain machines such as light and sound devices, or through consistent training processes, the Theta state can be attained. Most people are unable to do this consciously. Because it exists on the fine line of sleep, it is difficult to maintain the state without falling into sleep. This is the main reason we use the light and sound relaxation system at each of the Positive Changes Hypnosis

Centers. The machine trains the brain to move from the wide awake state into the intuitive and inventive states of the mind. This allows our clients to spend less time concerned if they are "hypnotized" and more time focusing the incredible power of the mind on the results they want in their life.

4. Delta State (The Unconscious Mind).

(4 to 0 cycles per second) Once the brainwave pattern of delta is reached, the subject is asleep. This is the place of dreams and visions that no one has quite been able to define. Delta is not generally used in hypnosis, but it is possible to communicate with a sleeping person using hypnotic techniques. We call this part of the mind "unconscious" because the subject is totally unaware of his or her outside environment.

At times a subject will appear to move from a state of deep relaxation into sleep and then awaken later. There has never been a case where someone was placed in the hypnotic state and then was unable to return. He or she would simply fall into a natural sleep and would soon awaken normally as if having received a deep, relaxing sleep.

Many of history's most successful inventors, such as Albert Einstein, functioned in the Alpha brainwave pattern far more often than in the Beta realm. In the Alpha and Theta brainwave rhythms, there is a noticeable release of stress, strain and frustration. You will want to inform your clients that they are, indeed, going into a specific state which is perhaps a bit out of phase from the conscious everyday Beta – wide awake – state.

Poet and playwright, Goethe (1749-1832) and composer, Chopin (1810-49) were both students of hypnosis at the University of Strasbourg. Additionally, Thomas Edison (1847-1931), Nikola Tesla (1856-1943) and Henry Ford (1863-1947) all reported using trance-like states to inspire their imagination.

Testing your subjects will give you the information necessary for a successful hypnotic session. Remember, hypnosis is a selective mind state. You are now ready to get the feel for placing yourself or another into that state. The following dialogue is designed for you to either read to someone or to speak into a tape recorder.

You will want to become aware of your voice at this point. Listen closely to the tone and cadence of your voice so that you begin to include the hypnotic tone and tempo that is a

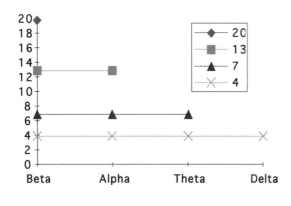

part of the hypnotic session. It takes practice, but as you use your voice, you will begin to articulate in a smooth and comfortable way so that others can follow along and be soothed by its sound. Recording these dialogues on tape and then playing them back is an excellent way to monitor your voice and articulation.

HOW DO YOU INDUCE ALPHA AND THETA BRAINWAVE ACTIVITY?

Begin by directing yourself or the subject to get into a comfortable position, either sitting in a comfortable chair or lying down. Then have the subject look at a specific spot on the ceiling or a wall. The purpose of having the subject focus on one particular spot is to create selective thinking. This is what is needed to get the subject to concentrate on your voice and allow the thoughts of the day to drift away.

Dialogue

Take a moment and become aware of a spot, any spot at all, and notice the lightness and darkness of that spot… and, as you do this, your eyelids are getting heavier and heavier but I want you to keep them open… keep them open for as long as you can.

As you continue to look at that spot, try to keep your eyes open, finding that the harder you try the more difficult it becomes and the more enjoyable it feels. Each time you practice focusing on a spot with the intention of going into hypnosis, it gets easier for you. Your eyelids continue to get heavier and heavier, and a feeling of wellbeing and peace begins to fill you up. I want you to try to keep your eyes open... Noticing the harder you try, the more difficult it becomes. But you continue to try to keep the eyes open.

Place into that spot the ideal you with all skills and all abilities. Your eyes continue to get heavier and heavier, and you try to keep them open. Soon, and very soon indeed, you will find your eyes closing... It's just too much work.

As your eyes close now, you will find yourself drifting into a dreamy-drowsy feeling of peaceful sleep. Now, just let your eyes close... comfortably relaxed... just let go... letting go of all thoughts, all cares, all anxieties of the day. There is no reason to listen to other sounds... There is no reason to listen to other voices... Focus on my voice and allow all other sounds to cause you to relax and go deeper.

From here become aware of your body... and as you do, allow each and every part of your body to go loose, limp and completely relaxed. In fact, you are going so relaxed... so completely relaxed that the seconds are like hours, the hours are like days and the days become weeks. Allow yourself this time to relax, releasing all conscious thoughts and cares of the day to drift away. Allow the feelings of peace, tranquility and spaciousness to enter into your mind.

From here, move into your imagination where you can begin to build a place around you... a place where you can drift away on a personal vacation... a vacation that will allow you to return with a fresh attitude about life and about your world... a healthy new attitude that will bring you more of what you want... just when you want it the most. In a moment my voice will pause and when it does you will find the seconds will become hours and the hours will become days. At that time you will project your mind into this vacation place. When my voice returns it will not startle you at all. In fact, it will place you into a deeper and more relaxed place in consciousness... It will be from that place that your new attitude will begin to grow and prosper, becoming reality for you upon awakening... and this is so... (Pause.)

Now as you relax and slowly return to this room, you will find that you can return only as slowly as you can incorporate the new attitude into your life... your world... and your experience. Each time that you practice self-hypnosis you will receive greater benefits... Each time you will go deeper and deeper. I will now count from one to five and at the count of five your eyes will open, you will feel wide awake and in perfect health... natural and normal in every way... 1... 2... 3... 4...5. Eyes open, wide awake and in perfect health... and this is so.

"What you get by reaching your destination is not as important as what you become by reaching your destination."

DR. ROBERT ANTHONY

Chapter Three

Neuro-Linguistic
Programming

A natural connection exists between **Neuro-Linguistic Programming** (NLP) and hypnosis, creative visualization and imagery as they relate to the use of Psycho-Linguistics in helping yourself or other people attain desired outcomes.

"Self-Talk" is the newest fad in self-help and is probably the fastest growing method of change technology. It involves a variety or combination of methods from spoken affirmations to scripting and dialoging. Self-talk is directed at accessing the old tape programs that were established throughout childhood and replacing them with new, more appropriate messages that better serve the individual. Self-talk is also an extension of NLP, which will be discussed more specifically during the section about auditory changes in hypnosis.

It is my belief that the terms *"imagery," "visualization"* and *"hypnosis"* are often improperly used and misrepresented. By this I mean to say that all states are in essence the same and for our purpose here these terms will be used interchangeably. NLP has taken imagery methods to the next level, and the founders of NLP have done a fine job of outlining the visualization process as the principal component of sub-modality work *(defined later in this chapter)*. In the section defining visual processing, I will cover the use of imagery more thoroughly.

As NLP founder Richard Bandler said, *"Everything is hypnosis or nothing is hypnosis."* Even though many people have tried to call these processes by different names (*visualization, imagery, self-talk, affirmations*) it really boils down to the same basic ingredients – those found in hypnosis. To paraphrase an old adage, *by any other name, a rose is still a rose.* So it is with hypnosis.

Prayer is another method that seems to have been left out of most therapy programs, whether private counseling, books or seminars. I feel this is mostly because of the wide variance in religious preferences. The way in which someone prays is extremely personal. To ease this sensitive issue, I simply recommend that people pray within the guidelines of their own faith. Those who have no particular religious inclination are asked to consider the possibility that something greater than them is at work in the universe. We have adopted the philosophy of Alcoholics Anonymous – an individual person in and of his or her self probably cannot change, but with the help of this universal power, all things are possible.

WHAT IS NEURO-LINGUISTIC PROGRAMMING (NLP)?

Perhaps it is best to explain what NLP is by relating just how it all came about. The founders of the process that is today known as NLP, Richard Bandler and John Grinder, conducted a nearly life-long study of successful therapists and trainers, their techniques and methods of communication with clients, and just what brought about consistently positive outcomes. The patterns of NLP evolved out of that quest. These patterns are rooted in linguistics and non-verbal communication. They are structured so anyone with the desire to succeed can follow the guidelines and achieve a similar level of success.

It is not the purpose of this book to fully define or teach you NLP. There is an abundance of books available that cover the theory and principles quite effectively. My intention is to show you, in text format, how I have taken what I learned in my training with several masters of NLP, combined it with the processes of hypnosis, imagery, creative visualization, self-talk and accelerated learning, and converted it into a successful system for helping people achieve their outcomes.

For our context in the Positive Changes Hypnosis Centers model, there was one flaw with NLP techniques, as they stood alone. Within the NLP structure, the founders created their own language; a terminology they decided was best suited for their method of teaching their approach to others. However, these language patterns became awkward outside the NLP world. Since most people seeking training have no knowledge of NLP, we found it necessary to adapt the language to fit their needs. One of my goals for Psycho-Linguistics is to give the patterns of NLP a degree of simplicity and contextualization for the hypnotist.

You will find a list of excellent books on NLP listed in the back of the text. These books are not required reading for Psycho-Linguistics to work for you, they are simply well-written books that will help you expand your knowledge if that is what you desire. If you would like to know more about NLP after reading Psycho-Linguistics, please note the books listed in the bibliography.

MAJOR PRESUPPOSITIONS OF NLP & PSYCHO-LINGUISTICS

Although there will be exceptions to all of these presuppositions, they are a useful starting place for communication and serve as the framework for every pattern of Psycho-Linguistics. After incorporating the guidelines into my private hypnosis sessions, I found my modest practice flourishing into a thriving business. Our referral rate more than tripled and the franchise is now expanding throughout North America.

1. Communication is redundant.

People are always communicating in all three major representational systems (*visual, auditory, and kinesthetic/feelings*). When you figure out the system an individual is accessing, you can present your information through that same channel so he or she will feel comfortable using it.

2. The meaning of your communication is the response that you elicit.

Communication is not about what you intend to relay, nor is it about saying the right words. Rather, it is about creating an experience and eliciting a response from the listener. The bottom line is the response you invoke. You must know where you are going so you will know when you get there. Psycho-Linguistics provides clearly defined outcomes that lead to successful communication.

3. People respond to their perception of reality, not to reality itself.

Psycho-Linguistics is the science of changing perception – not reality. It seems that when the perceptions are changed, reality will follow suit. In other words, when that which is changed is also that which is most constant, a new reality is defined. I have a favorite saying I often use with clients, *"If you want a constant change, change what is most constant – you."*

4. People work perfectly.

No one is wrong or broken. Thanks to this one short statement, hypnotists no longer need to endlessly explain to clients why hypnosis works. As an example, a good number of the clients we see each day at Positive Changes Hypnosis Centers come to us to stop smoking. I tell these people they have trained themselves to smoke so well that they now need my help to get them to stop. This typically brings a surprised look, but it is a truth with which they usually can relate. I then give them the spark of possibility, *"What if that part of you, the one that trained you so well to be a smoker, could be retrained to do something useful and beneficial?"* This is usually gladly accepted. It is not bad to have an addictive personality as long as you are addicted to good things, such as exercising, eating healthy foods and enjoying life.

5. People always make the best choice available to them at the time, although there are often better choices.

How many times have you said to yourself, *"If only I could go back in time and make a different decision"?* Wouldn't it be great if you could bring the wisdom of the future back with you to the present? Although this is not, technically, what occurs in hypnosis, in a sense it is true. You are going ahead in time through your imagination. The future you perceive is then stored as your past and you almost automatically begin to make choices with the newly updated information.

6. Every behavior is useful in some context.

In the world of NLP, this is a simple step called *reframing*. It involves finding out where and when a given behavior is useful, even if it is not necessarily positive. At times you really have to stretch it, but when you begin to look at a problem as an asset, something shifts in the mind, and it seems to lose its unconscious power over you. You are then free to make new choices that are as immediate and hopefully more appropriate.

7. Choice is always better than no choice.

Have you ever noticed how wild animals react when they are trapped in a corner with no place to turn? Isn't that just the way we act when mental or physical stress has us trapped, as if there is no way out when, in fact, there could be many solutions to our dilemma? At times just becoming aware of the obvious choices is all a person needs to successfully change behaviors that might have been with him or her since early childhood.

8. Anyone can do anything.

If one person can do something, it is possible to model it and teach it to anyone else. In the circles of NLP, this is known as *modeling*. It is the study of the internal states of consciousness and making changes within them to support the outcome that is desired.

9. People already have all the resources they need.

What people lack, unfortunately, is access to these resources at appropriate times and places. Psycho-Linguistics gives the hypnotist skills not only for asking the right questions, but also for noticing reactions, so that, when the appropriate response has been elicited, you can move on to making it a permanent and positive part of the person's life. You can't have a problem without a solution, and you can't have a solution without certain problems. Success or failure is based on one's ability to choose the solution with the least number of problems.

10. There is no such thing as failure, only feedback.

Every response can be utilized. This was the motivation that started my research into which aspects of NLP, hypnosis or any other change technology would actually work in a private, one-on-one setting. Surprisingly, the methods didn't have to work perfectly for me to use them. I could pick and choose, combine and modify them all, discovering which worked best for each personality.

11. Anything can be accomplished by anyone if the task is broken down into small enough chunks.

Quite appropriately, this is termed *chunking*. Most people tend to do either all or nothing. Unfortunately, far too many choose to do nothing. It is with this in mind that I often use the statement, *"A little bit of something is certainly better than a whole lot of nothing."*

HOW DO YOU ESTABLISH RAPPORT?

The first benefit I gained from NLP came in the form of rapport techniques that put me in control of the communication almost immediately. Sure, both hypnosis and psychology talk about rapport, but NLP takes it one step further. You don't have to wait for rapport to develop; you can plan for and produce rapport through a series of successful processes that I will outline for you here.

DEFINITION: Rapport

To be in agreement or alignment with another; meeting a person on their own level by using familiar words and matching body language; verbal and nonverbal matching.

Have you ever met someone and felt an instant kinship with that person? Perhaps the two of you seemed to instantly click, and the communication flowed easily and naturally. Perhaps it even felt as if you could spend hours just talking with that person, as if you had known him or her all your life.

On the other hand, have you ever met a person with whom you

could never quite get on the same wavelength? Communication may have been stilted with long silences and sentences started but not finished. Such stiff communication may have ultimately evolved into feelings of frustration or dislike for that individual.

These two types of communication are at opposite ends of the spectrum, and you will most likely encounter every type in between. What if you could have taken control of the communication with the "difficult" person? What if you knew how to get on that person's wavelength? Most likely the conversation would have ended with a totally different outcome – the outcome you wanted!

No matter the method of change technology chosen, all communication and behavior change happens through rapport, either on a conscious or unconscious level. There are several different styles for building and maintaining rapport. Admittedly, it is best to learn these techniques through one of our hands-on training sessions or our hypnotist internship program. However, I will do my best to outline them here so you can understand their importance and begin to benefit from their use.

WHAT ARE PHYSICAL MATCHING AND PHYSICAL MIRRORING?

In watching the most successful communicators, negotiators and mediators, you will see something special about their body posture. One of their hidden secrets to open communication is the matching and mirroring of body language.

For the most effective communication, choose to stand or sit in the same position as the person with whom you are talking. For example, if that person is sitting back with legs crossed and arms folded, you will sit in an identical position. Psychologists use this tool to make their patients more comfortable about opening up to them. Use this technique in all your communication – you will be quite amazed with the results.

You need not be concerned that the person will notice you mimicking his or her stance. Only at the other-than-conscious level will he or she notice your imitated behavior, and this will be as a mirror image.

People are comfortable with their own self-image and, since your body position looks similar, you become non-threatening. The person becomes comfortable with you and begins to relax – the barriers come down and the communication begins to flow.

You can learn to take physical matching to the degree of the most effective communicators by studying matching through practice and repetition. Start out consciously and then let it flow to the unconscious level.

WHAT IS AN EXAMPLE OF PHYSICAL MATCHING?

I once had a client who was an excellent example for the application of matching. "Scott" was never completely aware of the world around him and to many he seemed rather obnoxious. He is what is known in the world of NLP as an *internal processor;* which means he thought everything going on in his inner mind was what was actually happening in the outer world. Therefore, he was unaware of other people's basic needs and his own, often inappropriate, communication. Scott proved to be a highly intelligent fellow, but he had a limited ability for communicating his knowledge to others.

If you watched Scott from a distance, however, you could tell there were many things he could have done differently to gain rapport with others. He seemed to have an inborn ability of breaking rapport instead of gaining or maintaining it.

One day Scott came to my office. He was anxious and upset, and asked me if I could help him to acquire a new job. His hope was that, through hypnosis, I could help him gain his self-confidence, self-esteem, self-worth and so on. But what I found out was that, more than anything else, Scott needed some essential conscious skills – basic rapport skills. These are the skills that would allow him to make inroads into the interviewer's other-than-conscious awareness. People in a position of hiring generally hire those with similar qualities to their own.

I started by testing Scott and we found he was a very good hypnotic subject. He was able to take direct suggestions and utilize them immediately. During his visits, we took him through role rehearsals and practiced the interview. Using guided imagery, I gave him the post-hypnotic suggestion that, when he went into an interview, he would put himself into *"state,"* which meant he would begin to think of himself as successful, with the ability to speak and react appropriately. I worked with his other-than-conscious mind and made an agreement that, during an interview, he would match the interviewer's physical posture, breathing sequence, and the tone and tempo of his or her voice.

This would all be done without Scott's conscious mind knowing it. It was certainly okay if Scott wanted to do it consciously as well, but it was all set up on an other-than-conscious level so it could be relaxing to him and appear natural, thus staying outside conscious awareness of the interviewer.

Scott came directly to my office from the interview. He was more excited than I had ever seen him. He got the job. For the first time in his life, Scott had enjoyed a job interview. He said the employer had actually sat and chatted with him for some time after they discussed the position. The employer decided to hire Scott for the position on the spot.

Unfortunately, less than a week after his successful interview, I found Scott back in my office, this time with a deep frown on his face. *"What happened?"* I asked.

"I was fired," was his sullen reply.

Once Scott landed the job, he neglected to practice the techniques and repeat them on the job and in his everyday life. The interviewer liked Scott and experienced a comfortable rapport with him. He felt that Scott was a person who could learn and perform the job efficiently. When Scott got into a situation with his immediate supervisor, however, he reverted back to his old behaviors.

Scott needed to work on learning and practicing these skills on a conscious as well as other-than-conscious level. NLP is best known for conscious improvement that can have an immediate impact. These are the same conscious level skills best utilized by sales people – the non-verbal communication skills of matching, mirroring and rapport that allow you to pace and lead a prospect to the sale.

In truth, are we not selling ourselves everyday, all day long? Doesn't it make sense that the more skills, abilities, and resources you have for gaining and maintaining rapport, and for leading people where you want them to go, the more successful you will be in the world in general?

HOW DO YOU DEFINE MATCHING AND MIRRORING?

Physical Matching

When you feed back what you see as the external state of another person, you are using physical matching. Matching is an interactive skill used to gain rapport with another individual. Examples of physical matching include using the same gestures as the other person, or copying his or her voice tone and tempo.

Figure 9. Example of Physical Matching

Figure 10. Example of Physical Mirroring

Physical Mirroring

Feeding back in mirror image (opposite) what you see as the external state of another person is physical mirroring. Mirroring involves reflecting back another person's physical patterns of behavior. Mirroring is most often accomplished through body posturing.

Cross-Over Mirroring

Using one aspect of your behavior to match a different aspect of the other person's behavior is the basis of cross-over mirroring. Examples include adjusting your voice to match the rhythm of the other person's breathing; pace eye blinks with your finger movements; pace voice tempo with the nodding of your head.

Figure 11. Example of Cross-Over Mirroring

WHAT ARE TYPES OF PHYSICAL MATCHING?

A. Body posture (whole, half, part body matching) – *Sitting or standing – Body angle, stance; Position of arms, hands, legs and feet; Position of head and shoulder angles.*

B. Gestures – *Hand movements; Arm movements; Head movements; Body movements such as shrugs, body shifting, or head nodding.*

C. Breathing – *Fast or slow; Upper, middle or lower chest; Through the nose or mouth.*

D. Voice – *Tempo – fast or slow; Tonality – high or low; Timbre – deep or high; Intensity – excited or relaxed; Volume – loud, medium or soft.*

E. Facial expressions – *Facial Appearance: eye blinks, smile, mouth opened or closed, scowl or frown, puckered lips, wrinkled nose, and raised eyebrows.*

One excellent method of practicing rapport skills, and matching in particular, is to begin noticing the actions of the people around you. Restaurants or social settings are the most opportune places to observe body cues. You can discreetly practice matching the movements of those close to you. You will soon notice that, although the imitations seem obvious to you, those around you will be totally unaware of what you are up to.

In no way does the single technique of rapport sum up the benefits NLP brought to modern hypnosis, but rapport is the basis on which all therapy needs to stand. Without rapport nothing else can be achieved.

Rapport can be gained in many ways, but by far the most useful in change therapy is the ability, through observing eye movements, to structure communication in any given individual's lead system.

WHAT ARE LEAD SYSTEMS?

We each have preferences for how we like information presented to us. This is termed your LEAD SYSTEM:

Some like to SEE what you mean...	VISUAL
Some like to HEAR your idea...	AUDITORY
Some like to EXPERIENCE or FEEL what you are talking about...	KINESTHETIC

We also have preferences for the way we evaluate and analyze information:

Some decide by how things LOOK to them...	VISUAL
Some decide by how things SOUND to them...	AUDITORY
Some decide by how things FEEL to them...	KINESTHETIC

Generally, people take in information and communicate in all systems. People can have one kind of preference for gathering information, and another kind for interpreting it. For example:

LOOKING at a new car and then buying it because it FEELS right.

You will find the client much more receptive if your ideas are presented in the way he or she prefers. So how, you might ask, do I know what a person's preference is? Fortunately, most people will give you cues that are quite obvious when you know what you are looking for.

Have you ever heard the term, *"The eyes are the mirror to the soul?"* There is a great deal of truth to this statement. By watching the sequences of eye movement, you will soon discover a pattern. By simply observing this pattern, you will learn just how that person gets to *"yes"* – the mystery is solved!

WHAT IS EYE ACCESSING?

When people are in the process of communicating, there are definite physical signs that reflect how they are processing data.

When you ask someone a specific question, he or she will begin to access memories, thoughts or ideas to formulate a response. His or her eyes will automatically move in a prescribed manner in order to create or retrieve the information. This eye movement will give you the information you need to respond back in the same lead system. Chances are good that your response will then be accepted as presented.

WHAT ARE THE PHYSICAL CUES TO VISUAL PROCESSING?

If you ask a question that requires access to a visual answer, the eyes will usually look up to the right or left.

Although there are exceptions, we can generally say that eyes looking up to the right or left will indicate the person you are watching is processing visually. This does not necessarily mean, however, that this person is a visual access person. This will be covered in more detail later in this chapter.

In order to access visual processing, it is necessary to ask a question that evokes a visual answer. A question that involves sound or feeling will not work.

WHAT ARE VISUAL PREFERENCE WORDS?

- *I SEE what you mean.*
- *I can VISUALIZE it.*
- *That LOOKS good to me.*
- *Let me get a PERSPECTIVE.*
- *I drew a BLANK.*
- *I need to FOCUS in on that.*

HOW DO YOU IDENTIFY VISUAL PROCESSING?

The eyes tell you when the person is LOOKING for information or VISUALIZING. They may be accessing a remembered or constructed image or creating a picture. When eyes are staring into space it is also a sign of visual access. Squinting or blinking can also indicate visualization. Blinking can indicate punctuation as well.

BREATHING – *Shallow breathing high in the chest*

TONE AND TEMPO – *High pitched, nasal tone and/or quick bursts of words in fast tempo*

MUSCLE TONE – *Tension in the shoulders and stomach*

HAND AND ARM POSITIONS – *Finger pointing or arm extensions*

SKIN COLOR – *Pale or waning color*

EXERCISE: BUILDING VISUAL ACUITY

Directions: *Walk into a room of your house and look around for about ten seconds. Then walk into another room and write down everything that you remember seeing in that room.*

Objective:

- *To increase visual acuity*
- *To increase observation skills*

WHAT ARE THE PHYSICAL CUES TO AUDITORY PROCESSING?

When auditory processing is taking place, the subject's eyes will move toward the ears, either left or right. It is almost as if the brain is listening to the data.

WHAT ARE AUDITORY PREFERENCE WORDS?

- *I HEAR what you are saying.*
- *Your idea SOUNDS good to me.*
- *Now that's an EARFUL.*
- *That story RINGS A BELL.*
- *I can't tell you where I've HEARD that before.*

HOW DO YOU IDENTIFY AUDITORY PROCESSING?

The eyes will tell you whether the person is recalling sounds or conversations, or constructing new ones. The eyes will usually look either directly to the right or left. Often *"shifty eyes"* relate to an auditory access person. Also, when a person is looking down and to the left he or she is probably carrying on an internal dialogue (talking to oneself).

BREATHING PATTERN – *Even breathing in the diaphragm or with the whole chest, often with a prolonged exhale*

TONE AND TEMPO – *Clear resonant tone and an even, rhythmic tempo*

MUSCLE TONE – *Even muscle tension, minor rhythmic movements*

HAND AND ARM POSITIONS – *Hands and arms folded, counting fingers, fingers in telephone position all indicate internal dialogue*

EXERCISE: LETTING GO

1. *Think of a "negative" voice. Perhaps you will recall a voice from the past or a voice pitch that is irritating to you. Imagine the pitch of that voice slowly going higher and higher until it is out of your range of hearing. Imagine you can place it on the moon. You know it's there; it's just out of your hearing range.*

2. *Think of that "negative" voice once again and imagine the pitch going lower and lower until it is out of your hearing range. At the same time, imagine it slowing down and moving deeper and further into the earth until it is at the very center.*

3. *When you bring the voice up, are you able to hear it in the same way? If so, repeat the process. Each time, leave the voice at different ends of the spectrum, from speeding it up and placing it on the moon to slowing it down and placing it in the center of the earth.*

The purpose of this exercise is to allow your mind to re-present the auditory information in a new way. If you give the mind all options, which means the option of going very low to a stop or very high until out of your hearing, then the brain will store it in the most appropriate way for you. Since the negative voice is not a voice you would want to have in your future, the brain, knowing this and always making the best decision, will store it as *hypermnesia,* or out of your hearing. This is the selective ability to remember what you want to remember when you want to remember it. In actuality, we do this all the time without knowing it.

This technique of *letting go* is an appropriate one to be used with many cases of unconscious overeating, such as someone who hears an internal voice from the past relating certain beliefs about food.

A young woman by the name of "Alice" came in to see me for weight loss. She was a bubbly, enthusiastic and positive-minded young woman. Unfortunately, however, once she started eating she just couldn't seem to stop until all of the food was gone.

I started by asking her just how she knew to continue eating the food on her plate. She said that she recognizes when it is appropriate to stop eating, but later realizes that all of the food disappeared anyway. At this point, she had no idea how this was happening to her.

There were a couple of different strategies we could set into place. First, we could build a conscious approach of putting less food on her plate. This strategy worked to some extent, except that no matter what amount of food was on her plate, whether dining in a restaurant or eating with friends, she would continue to eat until every bite was consumed.

Our next step was to use a process of modeling to discover the sub-modalities that were creating the eating behavior. What we discovered was that, deep within her mind, while she was consuming food, she would hear her mother, grandmother and other voices of authority from her childhood telling her, *"You must eat all of the food on your plate! There are children in Africa starving to death! How can you be so wasteful?"*

As an adult, these voices are no longer relevant on the conscious level, but the other-than-conscious mind doesn't discern usefulness. It accepts all information as truth and only knows how to act out of habit. So Alice needed a way to *re-present* her beliefs about food to her other-than-conscious mind so that, whatever the intention, it could be met in a new way. In this case the word *re-present* refers to giving the other-than-conscious mind a new way to present information to the conscious mind based on new beliefs and experiences.

For Alice, the intention of the voice was a constant reminder that, if she continued to eat until her plate was empty, her mother would discontinue admonishing her and would praise her for finishing her food. Therefore, she built a positive intention out of a negative behavior, or what turned into a negative behavior as she got older and her body's metabolism could no longer keep up.

Bringing the "mother voice" up to a high pitch to the point where she couldn't hear it, and then to the low point where it was dissipated, re-presented the information to her other-than-conscious mind. Her mind, now knowing this voice was no longer current, changed the way the voice was stored, rendering it irrelevant. Alice's eating patterns changed allowing her to return to a healthy and normal weight. To Alice, it felt natural and effortless.

Naturally, there were other Psycho-Linguistics techniques and patterns incorporated, but I do believe this was the key for Alice. If you can help someone find his or her key issue to overcoming a behavior pattern or an addiction, it can start a landslide of change. So, this technique sets the stage for change, and, at times, can inspire the entire change.

WHAT ARE THE PHYSICAL CUES TO KINESTHETIC PROCESSING?

When accessing kinesthetically, you are accessing feelings. When a person is looking down and to the right, he or she is usually getting in touch with feelings and emotions.

WHAT ARE KINESTHETIC PREFERENCE WORDS?

- *I FEEL that we have made a great breakthrough.*
- *Let me get a HANDLE on what you're talking about.*
- *You've given me a SOLID understanding of your point.*
- *Please TACKLE this assignment as soon as you can.*
- *I haven't been able to GRASP the concept.*

HOW DO YOU IDENTIFY KINESTHETIC PROCESSING?

Eye movement for the kinesthetic processor involves looking down and to the right. Eighty percent of all people tested looked down and to the right for accessing emotions and to judge their physical state.

BREATHING PATTERN – *Deep breathing in the lower stomach area*

TONE AND TEMPO – *Low, deep voice quality; voice may also be "breathy." Tempo is slow with long pauses.*

MUSCLE TONE – *A great deal of movement and touching; relaxed musculature indicates an inward contact with feelings*

HAND AND ARM POSITION – *Palms turned upward and arms bent and relaxed*

SKIN COLOR – *Increased, fuller color*

"There is more to life
  than increasing its speed."

GANDHI

WHAT IS AUDITORY DIGITAL AND AUDITORY TONAL PROCESSING?

The auditory system consists of both pure sound and the spoken word. Since each is represented differently in the brain, NLP considers language (or auditory digital) a separate representational system from pure sound (or auditory tonal). The term "digital" is used because words are verbal symbols or digits.

As explained in the auditory section, when self-talk is occurring and the person is accessing internal dialogue, the eyes will move down and to your right. Since language is involved, this is also termed auditory digital.

HOW DO YOU IDENTIFY A PERSON'S LEAD SYSTEM?

The lead system is the first place a person will go to access information from the bio-computer (brain). You can think of this as the first number on a combination lock. You can't go any further toward opening a lock without knowing the first number. Watching the first position to which the eyes move when asked a neutral question identifies the lead system of an individual.

A neutral question is one that doesn't lead the person with the use of sensory-based language (visual, auditory or kinesthetic). An example of a sensory question would be, "What do you think of the color of that car?" You asked the person to process visually in order to identify the color of the car. A neutral question would be, "What do you like about that car?"

It is possible for educators to determine an individual's learning strategy through eye access identification. A teacher can determine a student's learning mode by watching him or her process a math problem. With this information, the teacher is better equipped to help the student understand mathematics.

Much of NLP is based upon research that identifies how people move their eyes in systematic directions depending upon the kind of thinking they are doing. In NLP these movements are called *eye accessing cues*. The Eye Accessing Chart indicates the kind of processing most people do when moving their eyes in a particular direction. Small percentages of people are reversed and will move their eyes in a mirror image to the chart. This is why *calibration* of each individual is so important.

To *calibrate* is to watch and read an individual's external state through observable behavior cues that relate to his or her internal state. People go through a variety of external changes during communication, which are indicative of the internal responses. Examples are small gesture movements, a change in the breathing rate, voice tone and tempo changes, eye position changes, and changes in body position, such as a tilt of the head.

Be aware that words are the poorest form of communication. It is essential to listen to the words spoken, but also pay attention to all the cues displayed by the individual. Remain focused on what is occurring externally.

The best way to use this chart is to imagine it superimposed over someone's face as if that person is looking back at you.

"The advertising industry is one of our most basic forms of communication and, allegedly, of information. Yet, obviously, much of this ostensible information is not purveyed to inform but to manipulate and to achieve a result – to make somebody think he needs something that very possibly he doesn't need, or to make him think one version of something is better than another version when the ground for such a belief really doesn't exist."

MARVIN E. FRANKEL

EYE ACCESSING CUES CHART

Vc – Visual Construct: The eyes move to this position when a person is creating an experience or imagining the future.

Vr – Visual Remember: The eyes move to this position when a person is recalling an experience or accessing the past.

Ac – Auditory Construct: The eyes move to this position when a person is constructing what to say or talking about the future.

Ar – Auditory Remember: The eyes move to this position when a person is recalling what was a said or accessing a past conversation.

K – Kinesthetic: The eyes move to this position when a person is getting in touch with inner feelings about an experience. This could be past or future.

Ad – Auditory Digital: The eyes move to this position when talking to oneself.

HOW DO CONVERSATIONS BECOME MISCOMMUNICATION?

As you become more aware of the non-verbal cues a person gives you, you will also notice how that person's verbal communication matches these outward signs. As you read over the following dialogue, ask yourself: Who wins in this conversation? Do these two have rapport? What modes of communication are being used here?

> SAM SALES: "I would like you to LOOK at this proposal. I'm sure you will SEE how it will give your customers a new VISION of your company."
>
> CANDY CONSUMER: "Yes, I FEEL there are some EXCITING points. But, I just can't get a HANDLE on how my clients will GRASP the concept."
>
> SAM SALES: "Perhaps you don't SEE the entire PICTURE. I realize it APPEARS a little VAGUE right now, but if you will allow me to DEMONSTRATE what my company can do for your company, I know we will SEE EYE to EYE."
>
> CANDY CONSUMER: "I need to GET IN TOUCH with my FEELINGS on this. Your proposal may change the entire FOUNDATION of our company. I need to FEEL COMFORTABLE with the whole concept. I'll TOSS IT AROUND in my mind and get back with you."

SAM SALES Is: ( ) Visual   ( ) Auditory   ( ) Kinesthetic

CANDY CONSUMER is: ( ) Visual   ( ) Auditory   ( ) Kinesthetic

---

Will SAM sell his "VISION" to CANDY? ( ) Yes   ( ) No

Who could benefit most from improved communication?
( ) SAM   ( ) CANDY   ( ) Both[7]

---

[7] Answers: Sal – Visual; Candy – Kinesthetic; Sell – No; Benefit – Both

It is not likely that SAM will sell his "VISION" or anything else to CANDY. It is as if they are speaking two entirely different languages. Who could benefit most from improved communication? Both. CANDY's job is to put her company in the best position for her customers and to help her company grow. By speaking the same language as the salesperson, she can get the most complete information and make the best decision.

Of course, SAM's livelihood depends on his ability to communicate to the buyer. If SAM had spoken in CANDY's language, she may very well have taken the time to get the details of his proposal. She may have been able to GET A HANDLE on his concept. These principles could mean the difference between success and failure.

HOW CAN YOU ENHANCE YOUR VERBAL COMMUNICATION?

The following exercises will help you understand how speaking in a person's *"language"* can help you gain access to his or her bio-computer and attain the results you want.

Start by imagining you are a real estate salesperson. Real estate agencies often report that the house clients describe and the one they actually buy are usually very different. The superior real estate salesperson will first uncover how a person processes data, thereby discerning the individual's buying strategy. The agent can then select a house that matches this buyer's "hidden" needs.

What are the features a sales agent will want to emphasize…

For a VISUAL person? – *Color, look, scenery.*

For an AUDITORY person? – *The quietness of the neighborhood. The sound construction. The nice conversations the family could have.*

For a KINESTHETIC person? – *The solid foundation. This is a concrete investment. The firm offer.*

Think about a certain place where you enjoy spending time. What is special about that place that makes you enjoy being there? Now think of a place where you just didn't like to be and could barely wait to leave. What was it about that place that was driving you away? Clearly, atmosphere alone can make or break rapport.

Imagine you are going on a first date and you want to make a good impression. What types of entertainment will this person enjoy?

For a VISUAL person – *A movie; a nightclub with flashing lights; a scenic trip in the country.*

For an AUDITORY person – *Listening to music; going to a concert; a talk in a nice restaurant.*

For a KINESTHETIC person – *Going for a walk; exercising; relaxing out in nature.*

In building a relationship, it is important to continually access the other person's lead system to strengthen the bond and anchor to each other. Think about how getting the right gift could make the difference.

Listed below is the kind of special gift you might buy for a significant other for his or her birthday.

For a VISUAL person – *Watch; picture; a flashy car or piece of jewelry.*

For an AUDITORY person – *A record or tape; concert tickets; a stereo.*

For a KINESTHETIC person – *Comfortable clothing; comfortable furniture; loose fitting jewelry.*

Establishing and maintaining communicative rapport is essential in any relationship. At times, we are placed into situations where rapport has been greatly diminished. This next question will help you understand the use of lead systems to rebuild trust and rapport.

Listed below is how you might apologize to a significant other.

For a VISUAL person – *Beautiful flowers; dinner in a classy restaurant; doing something he or she can see.*

For an AUDITORY person – *I want you to hear me say I'm sorry; I hope you can hear me out; I'm sorry for what I've said.*

For a KINESTHETIC person – *I know it's hard to handle but, I'm sorry; I'm sorry for grinding you the wrong way; give a big hug while saying, "I'm so sorry."*

WHAT IS ANCHORING?

In the most general sense, an anchor is any stimulus that elicits a consistent response. One of the major breakthroughs in NLP is the discovery that a person can elicit a conditioned response in a single attempt once that response is intentionally linked to a touch, word, gesture or tone.

There are signals or signs that you automatically react to in one way or another, such as the STOP sign. There are also certain cultural anchors to which most members of a particular culture will respond. In the United States we have: The American flag, the National Anthem, and red/yellow/green stop lights, as examples.

Anchors from one's own personal history are also powerful. As examples: The smell of bread baking reminds you of Sunday visits to Grandmother's house; the touch of leather against your hand reminds you of your favorite old leather jacket; or, the taste of cotton candy brings back memories from your first visit to the fair.

Music and songs are also anchors and often re-elicit sensory representations from the time when the tune was popular.

Advertising is possibly the best example of anchoring: *"The Real Thing,"* and *"How do you spell relief?"* are two good examples. The Nike corporation did such a good job of anchoring their logo symbol into our consciousness, their commercials no longer even show their name or product, yet we all know a Nike commercial when we see one, and people purchase more Nike athletic shoes than any other brand. These are just a few examples of how we are intentionally conditioned into specific responses.

When an individual is in an intense state, and a specific stimulus is applied simultaneously, then the two – stimulus and state – become neurologically linked. In the future, when the stimulus is applied, the intense state will result.

BASIC ANCHORING GUIDELINES

1. Put yourself and/or the person to be anchored into the desired state.

Establish a *full sensory anchor,* with all senses participating. Begin by recalling a situation or event that brings up the desired sights, feelings and sounds.

As an example, "Fred" was once a professional football player with a notable career behind him. After retirement, he wanted to become a successful salesman, but every time he picked up the phone he would start to feel as if he couldn't do it. He believed he didn't have the skill to make the sale. He would ask himself, "Why am I even doing this?" He began to recall his lofty career in football and feelings of falling short overcame him. What he didn't realize is that a sales career is nothing shabby. Some of the richest people in the world are in sales. **I had Fred close his eyes and imagine a time, to the best of his ability, when he was doing something very well.** Fred had been a running back, so I had him remember a time when he knew, without doubt, that if his play was called in the huddle, he would have the ability to carry it out. When Fred got into the football state, you could physically see the change. His face appeared visibly younger as a glow overcame him and a smile moved across his lips.

Now I could intensify the anchor. I asked him to step into the action. I began setting up the *Five-Tupple,*[8] which is an anchor with all five senses involved. I first had him visualize the experience internally. I had him imagine what was occurring around him; all that he could remember *seeing.* He could then begin to *hear* what he was saying to himself internally, and then what he was physically hearing at the time. Now he was able to access the *feelings* of the event. He began experiencing the feeling of the situation as if he were in that body

[8] Dilts. et al., Neuro-Linguistic Programming, 1980, Meta-Publications.

again, breathing the way he breathed at that time. I then had him add any *smells* or *tastes* that were present and would further anchor him into that positive experience. Fred was now experiencing a full-sensory recollection of the event. He was seeing, hearing, feeling, smelling and tasting the incident fully. I have now set a full-sensory anchor, ready to be placed into Fred's future sales career.

2. At the height of the experience, set the anchor.

The best anchor is a tactile one. This means to touch, preferably on the back of the hand or the shoulder. It is imperative that you explain the anchoring sequence to your clients before you ever touch them and that you anchor in a place that cannot possibly be misunderstood as an advance. Gauge the individual to find out whether it is appropriate to touch him or her.

There are, in fact, many different anchors. You can use tonal anchors with your own voice. For example, a minister who uses a certain emphasis while preaching to a congregation; such as using the word *"Jesus"* with conviction, is using a tonal anchor. Or, it could be the way a football or basketball coach uses the word *"breakdown."* By far the best anchor for the hypnotist's purposes, however, is the tactile one.

At the moment you notice the height of the experience, you will reach over and touch the subject. After you have made contact in an appropriate way and with an even pressure you will release it completely.

3. After the anchor is set,
that particular state is broken.

The subject is returned to full awareness of his surroundings. As an example suggestion, "Roll your eyes open and look around the room... notice the room around you." At times I will make an amusing comment or point out something noticeable within the room. It is also helpful to have your client shift his or her neurology with movement of the body so the anchor is not linked to any other experience. A simple suggestion to move the feet and hands will accomplish this shift.

4. Reactivate the anchor to test for responses:

Check for variances in skin color, breathing, body tension, posture, and movement. The test should elicit the original state for the anchor to be effective. Simply reach over and reactivate the anchor; touch the same place and then notice the reaction. If you need to strengthen the anchor, it is perfectly okay to build a stronger response at this time.

In later chapters, as we review the individual Psycho-Linguistics patterns, you will learn more about anchors and gain a better understanding of their usage. Anchoring is one of the primary tools of the Psycho-Linguistics practitioner.

WHAT IS A SUBMODALITY AND HOW DO YOU USE IT IN PSYCHO-LINGUISTICS?

All thinking takes place through one or more of the five sensory channels – visual (sight), auditory (sound), kinesthetic (touch or feel), olfactory (smell) and gustatory (taste).

The face is a reflection of what is occurring internally. Any sequence of images will produce the same external expression, whether through verbal or nonverbal behavior. This processing of image types, and the expressions it elicits, is what makes anchoring effective.

Submodalities are the internal characteristics in each modality (visual, auditory or kinesthetic) that together comprise the structure of an individual's experience. Internal submodalities can produce external changes, and vice versa. In other words, it is the way in which we process the world around us through internal pictures, sounds and feelings. Once you know how someone processes the world, you can work with that internal process or even change it if necessary. An example would be if a client has a see-food-eat-food strategy. As a hypnotist, you use submodality shifts to get the client to process seeing food differently. One example would be to have them see the food, ask themselves if they are truly hungry and then imagine what they will feel like after consuming that food.

HOW DO YOU ELICIT AND USE SUBMODALITIES?

There is no better way to elicit submodalities than simply asking the subject to access them. As an example:

Question: *Go inside and find a positive memory. When you find it, let me know.* When the subject verifies the positive memory, move to the next step.

Question: *Is the picture in color or black and white? Is it moving or still? Are you in the picture or watching it from a distance? Is there sound or is it silent?* You can ask any question relating to the description of the experience or desired outcome through the sensory channels.

If the positive image is in black and white, suggest…

> *What happens if you make it colorful? Imagine a Hollywood producer is colorizing the experience. Is that better or worse?*

If the answer is better, keep it there. If not, return it to black and white. In my experience, no client has ever wanted positive memories stored in black and white.

Next Step: *Imagine the sound as if it is surrounding you and your favorite music plays in the background. Is this better or worse?*

I have never known clients to not enjoy music in the background of their favorite experiences.

Next Step: *Imagine stepping into the experience. Breathe the way you were breathing, see what you were seeing, imagine all the smells… really get a flavor for this experience.*

At this point, a smile usually starts across the face of the client and you know he or she is having a great time.

You can do the same thing above in reverse to eliminate a negative experience. I like to make them black and white and place them behind the client as a part of the past. I suggest that they look at those past experiences as learning experiences. With this knowledge, they can move forward into the future knowing they have learned that lesson well and never have to repeat it.

Finding and using submodalities can be much more sophisticated than this, as is demonstrated in many NLP books. However, after working with thousands of clients, I have come to the conclusion that submodality information is most useful in strategy intervention and modeling processes, which is not the focus of this text.

Keep in mind that all the patterns of Psycho-Linguistics are designed to change, delete or distort the past information and to enhance, clarify and present the new information in a more appropriate light. As hypnotists we teach people *how* to think, not *what* to think. Most people are unaware of how they can perform maintenance on their mind so they feel good for no reason at all.

Again, the purpose of this book is not to be a text about NLP or hypnosis, but rather to outline the Psycho-Linguistics patterns that draw from the best of each. NLP has strongly influenced all aspects of my life. If the patterns of Psycho-Linguistics interest you, I urge you to further your training within these realms. Contact an NLP professional in your area, preferably someone trained through one of the recognized NLP educational programs.

If you are interested in a career in hypnosis, you may want to consider the internship program offered at your local Positive Changes Hypnosis Centers location. The best way to master these patterns and each of the nuances within them is to learn from the professionals who have mastered them before you.

"The test of a first-rate intelligence
is the ability to hold two opposed ideas
in the mind at the same time,
and still retain the ability to function."

F. SCOTT FITZGERALD, US novelist (1896-1940)

Chapter Four

Accessing the Hypnotic Mind

In my early years as a hypnotist, I began to ask these questions: What would my hypnosis sessions be like if I had the ability to access the minds of all other successful hypnotists? What if there was a universal mind to which I could *"tap in,"* so I would somehow know exactly the right words to say at just the right time? If it did happen, how would I know it? And, what if, by happening just once, it could repeat itself every time I went into a hypnosis session? What if, in each session, I could draw on a potential within myself that would guide the conversation, help me layout the best outcomes, and elicit the best response for my client?

What I discovered was that all of this could (and does) happen by simply gaining access to what I have come to call the *hypnotic mind.*

There is a reason you chose to pick up this book and read it at this precise moment. You have a desire that drew you to this book. The desire will vary from person to person, but for most it is either a desire to help yourself, to help others, or, as a practicing hypnotist, to find fresh, new ideas for enhancing your current techniques.

There is a genuine way to access all these possibilities. In hypnosis training they teach you to move into a state called *self-hypnosis.* NLP practitioners call it entering a *state of mind.* In the Silva Method, they direct you to *go to level.* For the hypnotist, I believe this state is most appropriately termed the *hypnotic mind.*

Your mind works best when you are specific. There is a specific place in each and every one of us that has chosen a people-helping profession – it is a place for compassion and for guiding others to solutions and wellbeing.

Your *hypnotic mind* is the part of you that needs to read this text and then review the information to ensure a natural flow of information whenever you need it.

There are some simple guidelines for accessing the *hypnotic mind*. Following these guidelines will give you full flexibility in using the *non-contextual* Psycho-Linguistics patterns.

By non-contextual, I mean that you don't have to know the context around a problem to help guide your client to a solution. This is in alignment with my belief that the hypnotist's job is to teach people *how* to think, not *what* to think.

Although I am teaching specific guidelines for success, you must be flexible if you wish to be effective with each individual personality. When people sit across from you and pour out their heart, soul, dreams and desires, you must be adaptable in using the Psycho-Linguistics patterns and techniques.

Plan to take what you read in this book and combine it with what you have read elsewhere, what you have seen in any film, heard on any tape, or learned at any seminar, and be willing to use all that you know to create your own patterns for success. This kind of creativity will keep you actively involved in your hypnosis sessions and, most importantly, will make being a hypnotist an exciting adventure.

When helping others to achieve change, it is necessary to put yourself into a receptive state. This is the state I call the *hypnotic mind.* A deep caring for people is almost always the driving force behind professions such as hypnotist, counselor, psychologist, nurse, or Neuro-Linguistic Programming practitioner. To be successful with others who have changes to make and problems to overcome, it is important that you get into that place of caring.

The following suggestions are written for you. Simply take a moment to read through them and then begin to use them in your daily life and activities. See how they impact your relations with others.

GUIDELINES FOR TAPPING INTO THE HYPNOTIC MIND

For this next exercise, you will need a recording device such as a cassette recorder or a compact disc recorder. You could also record this into your computer and play it back for personal use.

Speak clearly and naturally into the microphone. Unlike the hypnotist of old, there is no reason to use a theatrical voice. Imagine you are reading a loving message to someone you deeply care about. The resonating hypnotic voice will develop with time. Please note that when you see periods of ellipsis (...) this means that you pause by taking in a deep breath. There is no reason to rush the process.

Hypnotic Mind Script:

With your eyes comfortably closed, take in a deep cleansing breath... let it go with a sigh... Concentrate on breathing in deeply and breathing out completely... Notice that with each breath you take, you are going deeper and further inside... You are going inside your own mind.

As you let go of the external world, you become more and more aware of the inner world of your thoughts... Thoughts are more powerful than things, thoughts create things... As you become less and less aware of your body and become more and more aware of your mind, you are less concerned with external sounds... In fact, each time you practice using hypnosis, you find that outside sounds and influences only cause you to go deeper... deeper... deeper and deeper still, until you find the perfect level of relaxation for you.

From here I want you to create a room... This will be your training room. In this room you will learn to connect with and become a part of the hypnotic mind. From here you can review all books you have read... all classes you have attended... Everything you need to know, you do know in this space... in this time of deep and profound relaxation.

Imagine that there is a comfortable chair... a chair ten times more comfortable than any chair you have ever sat in. Find yourself settling into your chair... your chair of deep and profound relaxation. While in this chair you have access to all skills, all abilities, and all resources you would need to develop your connection with the hypnotic mind... Each time you will find yourself going deeper... deeper and deeper still.

From this inner place, notice how your mind works when you have all the information you need... when you know exactly what to say... and you say it with perfect tone and tempo. You might find it useful to recall a time with a family member or friend when you were having a conversation and it was flowing... flowing as naturally as water running down hill.

With this memory now available, imagine that you notice their breathing... and you immediately match their breathing and you notice that you relax and go deeper still... You notice when you are in rapport, and when you are out of rapport, and you make all the adjustments... Each time that you review a conversation in this manner you get better... better, better and better than the time before.

You notice the level of your body's relaxation... just moments ago you started the process... the process of connecting with the hypnotic mind... from here... if you don't mind, I would like you to go even deeper.

From this inner place, you notice in the conversation the words that they are using... you notice if those words are visual words, like look, see or bright... you notice if they are auditory words, like click, snap or do you hear me now?... you even get a gut feeling when they start using kinesthetic words like grasp, concrete or handle... Most importantly, you are learning to use their words back to them in a way that builds hypnotic rapport.

From this deep inner place... resting comfortably in your hypnotic chair... you notice how they move their eyes... Even as other parts of the conversation are happening in the room around you, you notice when their eyes move up, they could be accessing visual information, when their eyes move side to side, they could be accessing auditory information, when they look down, they could be talking to themselves or accessing feelings... You are becoming so aware of the nonverbal communication that you know exactly what to say and how to say it... Just let yourself go... let go and review this process.

*You have done this once. This means you have the memory of it...
And you can do it once again... This means you have done this twice
differently... Once, step by step, listening to each word that was said
and the second time by remembering it.... This means you have now
done this four times... wouldn't you agree?... Once when you listened
to the step-by-step process, second by reviewing it in your mind, then
twice again differently through this review process.*

*And because you are still listening to my voice, there is a part of you
that continues to remember how many times we have really done this
process... go inside and check it out... You've done it again... this
time differently... You have reviewed the complete process, which
means you've now practiced eight times...*

*By now you would probably agree that this is just too much work...
let's turn this process of learning over to the other-than-conscious
mind. That's the part of the mind that continues to learn even while
you do other things... Things that are very important, like beating
your heart... helping you to breathe.*

*While you continue to experience the benefits of deep relaxation, I
would like your conscious mind to go on a mental vacation. You go
wherever you want... you can be with whomever you would like to
be with... Take a moment to enjoy the journey, knowing that every
day and every way you are learning to use the Psycho-Linguistics
patterns to improve your life and the lives of others... And when you
have finished your mental vacation, slowly count yourself back up to
fully awakened consciousness... 1, become aware of the room that
you are in... 2, notice the feeling of wellbeing... 3, each time you are
capable of going this deep and then deeper... 4, with a perfect memory
and recall of the process so that you can do this all on your own...
and... 5, eyes open, wide awake... wide awake... feeling fine and in
perfect health... and this is so.*

By putting together a series of events that will take place like a
checklist and occur automatically, you are now incorporating the
hypnotic mind. As you listen to your Hypnotic Mind Script, and check

off the items in your mind, you will feel confident and prepared to do just what you need to do.

Let's take this a little further. Say an elderly woman comes to you to stop smoking after a 45 year-habit. Her life and motivations are much different from yours. However, through the use of these techniques, you will begin to see the world through her eyes, while retaining the integrity of your own ideas and visions. In other words, you view the client's world, or her map of it, and help her plot a course of success to where she wants to go – which is not necessarily where *you* want her to go. Always remember that she came to you because you have techniques and tools she believes will give her the ability to attain her goal.

In other words, keep a positive attitude about your client. Realize that all behaviors are positive. Behind every behavior there is a positive intention that your client is attempting to accomplish. Until now, however, it has been in an inappropriate way. Your job is to help her, through the visual, auditory and emotional channels, to change the way she responds to life. She needs a change that will fulfill her positive intention and convince her that, once and for all, absolutely and positively, it will improve her world.

While helping every client to make it through his or her day-to-day activities in new ways, it is imperative that you focus on behavior changes that are equally as *immediate and appropriate*. This means to help your client function within his or her existing world and to move through experiences with a positive mental attitude and with relaxation in mind and body.

From here you will take your client into the future. Thoughts of the days, the weeks and the months to come with this new, positive attitude should now be placed within the mind. This new perception of the future, along with the forecasting ability of the mind, will bring all the solutions into view.

Keep in mind that the power to change is within each person. You, as a hypnotist, hold the golden key for yourself alone. Each and every client who walks through your door already has their own golden key and the potential to change. Clients pay for a hypnotist's expertise because we are trained to teach them to use their keys and access change. It is your job to show these people how to use their keys and then hand them over. You are empowering your clients to go out into the world and create a better future.

WHAT IS HYPNOTIC RAPPORT?

The ability to ask the right questions, to build an awareness of the person's position and then to become one with him or her is known as *hypnotic rapport*. Once this rapport is established, the client can more readily be lead into a positive and more compelling state.

Hypnotic rapport is accomplished in a variety of ways. The most widely used method involves breathing with the same rhythm as another person. After you breathe like someone for a while, he or she will begin to feel a connection with you. It will be the feeling of *bonding*, but it will not be conscious. This unconscious bonding is the most important contact between you and your client.

Another way to build this common bond is to use the same lead system as your client. Whether that system is visual, auditory, or kinesthetic (emotional), even if it is different from your own, it is the most familiar to that individual. For example, a 25 year-old man has come to you because he has decided to start a college program, but is having difficulty recalling the information he is learning. His lead access is kinesthetic. This young man would probably find it very difficult to describe his problem to you.

What would happen if you began to ask him questions using his lead system? You would be able to help him access his own bio-computer because you will be in the position of controlling the conversation. He will automatically begin accessing through his feelings. You have not only developed rapport with this young man, but you are also in a position to elicit the information you need to direct the session to his desired outcome. Realize that there is a difference between controlling a person and controlling the session. You, as a hypnotist, can only control the session.

An individual's own tone and tempo is also a very familiar place within. If you begin using the same rate of speech and voice level, it will tap into a comfortable place inside of that person. In most cases, when an individual speaks rather quickly, he or she is accessing a visual mode of communication. If an individual's cadence of speech is rapid, and you respond with that same tempo and tone, the brain will hear it and assimilate it as if it was said within his or her own mind. *(Review Chapter Two.)*

Body language is a familiar term today, but most people don't realize the effect that a mutual body posture can have when building rapport in communication. If your client, say a young female who is not familiar with discussing her behaviors with a stranger, is sitting with her legs crossed and her hands clamped tightly in her lap, you can be certain that she does not yet feel comfortable with you. How do you persuade this young woman to open up to you? You can start out by positioning your body in her same posture and crossing your body in the same way. As the conversation goes on, begin to open your body up and uncross your limbs. More often than not, she will follow your lead and uncross her posture as well. Once her posture is open, she is more readily able to share with you and will be receptive to the information you are going to share. She is now in the right state of mind to accept the positive, new information.

These techniques will build hypnotic rapport; a level of trust that needs to occur for the person to accept what you are saying and place you in control of the session.

WHAT ABOUT ETHICS?

When using mind technology, whether it's hypnosis, Neuro-Linguistic-Programming, or psychology, there is an element of power that you have over the other person – it is your command over the communication. You will be able to persuade people, both consciously and unconsciously, to make changes to their thinking – sometimes without their awareness that the change occurred. However, the same rules apply with Psycho-Linguistics, or any other method of persuasion, as they do to hypnosis; *no one will be made to do anything they would not otherwise do.*

If you have picked up this book with the intention of gaining skills for controlling others in less than positive ways, this is not the mind technology for you. These techniques are designed for enhancement of the personality and you will find no brain-washing methods within these pages. All patterns work best when the person is motivated by positive outcomes.

I emphasize that a hypnotist does not have control over the other person, but does hold the ability to control the situation. Because you are learning to use and master vocabulary, as well as helping the other person to access information within his or her own mind, you surely are aware that there is an element of control. You are in control of the communication, which is only effective by virtue of the response it elicits.

Success lies within the communication that takes place between you and the subject. If success is occurring within that conversation, you can see, feel and hear that success. As you master the art of communication, success will soon become a day-to-day experience for you. You will be setting up such a powerful program within your mind that each day it will grow stronger than the day before.

The true promise of your mind is to take in all information, absorb it, calculate it, and then formulate a new future. This process will even carry over into your dreams so that every night as you drift off into sleep, in that state of dreamy drowsiness, your powerful mind will begin forecasting your next day, the next week and even the next month to come. It validates all information and puts it into motion for you. (Was that a direct hypnotic suggestion? I suppose so, since at the moment, you are reading my book and, therefore, I control the communication!)

WHAT IS YOUR "MOST PROBABLE FUTURE"?

Your most probable future is the future that is most likely to happen if all events and circumstances remain on their present course. If you ask the question, "Why are you overweight?" the response will have little to do with the results the client wants. There are many other reasons for keeping the word *"why"* out of a hypnosis session when utilizing these patterns. The main reason is that the question *"why"* gives the client access to an emotional response or other unnecessary programs; the proverbial *"bucket of worms."* If you want to spend hours listening to your client's explain all of their problems and situations, then ask the question, "*Why?*"

The reality is that the mind doesn't really care to worry about the patterns of the past. In fact, the mind is an expert at the past and the reasons "*why.*" What the client's mind does need to know is specifically what is going to be done, how it is going to get done, when it will be taken care of, with whom, and so on. The brain is a servo-mechanism. It only knows how to achieve goals. As you place the goals in the mind in a positive and appropriate way, the brain fills with awe and wonder and begins to build expectancy. In that building of expectancy, the brain will put the thoughts of the mind into motion. In actuality, no one really knows the full effect the mind can have on the body. You are empowering the mind for action; setting up a *most probable future* in which all desirable outcomes are fulfilled.

"*Why*" is not a word of empowerment. "*Why*" is an out. It is an excuse that is not used in any successful hypnosis session at our centers or in any other therapeutic session that has a positive outcome.

Keep in mind that you are seeking solutions and your mind and every client's mind wants to generate them. Whether you are using these techniques to help yourself or as a hypnotist for others, you need to place yourself and other people into a place of power. When you empower people around you, you become more powerful.

WHY DO YOU NEED AN OUTCOME FOR HYPNOTIC RAPPORT?

In building hypnotic rapport, there is one essential element that must be present and that is an *outcome*. Your mind must know the outcome you are striving to achieve for it to work properly. Your mind needs to recognize that the desired outcome will fulfill some underlying positive intention.

The following script is designed to help you integrate the "*patterns of hypnotic rapport.*" There is no need for you to answer them consciously, but when you finish, you may want to write them down or say them out loud. Simply sit back, relax into the hypnotic process and allow your mind to drift and wander as you ponder on each of the questions.

Outcome Script for Hypnotic Rapport

Go ahead and close your eyes... take in a deep full breath... let it go with a sigh... Continue to breathe in deeply and let it go completely. Today, with your eyes closed, you are going to rehearse ways to create outcomes... Outcomes will help you to organize your sessions with intent and purpose.

Since you have relaxed before, this time it will be easier... In fact, each time that you close your eyes with the intention of going into hypnosis, it will get easier and easier... You are becoming less concerned with outside sounds and more and more aware of the sound of my voice... Allow my voice to be centered midway between the right and left side of the brain... From there it will guide you into that relaxed comfortable room that you have created in the core of your mind... From there... if you don't mind... you slip into the chair and relax and go even deeper... deeper and deeper still. Soon, with just the thought of closing your eyes and entering into the relaxed state of hypnosis, you will go this deep and deeper with just a couple of deep breaths.

From here, your other-than-conscious mind will help you reach a goal today... With this thought, think of a specific step that you will take to accomplish that goal upon awakening... With that thought, let yourself go even deeper.

Imagine from here that you can communicate with this other-than-conscious part of yourself... Deep inside ask the question... Other-than-conscious Mind, will you be willing to bring these new behaviors and attitudes into reality so I can benefit from using them through the days, the weeks and the months to come... so that I might use them and integrate them into my world on a permanent and lasting basis?...

Each time that you practice this technique, you will have better internal communication... Each time your mind and its ability to communicate meaningful change into your life will only get better... better... better and better, every day in every way you are getting better.

From here notice the level of relaxation you have already attained... Just moments ago you closed your eyes; your body started the relaxation response... Each time you will go deeper.

At this deeper level of the mind, ask yourself the question... **Other-than-conscious Mind, will you guide me through a process of viewing how often I will need to display these behaviors before they become an active part of my personality? Will it happen today? Next week? Or, a month from today?** *... As you ponder the response from your other-than-conscious, it could come as a sound... perhaps as a feeling... you could even see the specific things that you will need to do.*

It is from here that you will listen to that other-than-conscious part of yourself when you ask the question. **Other-than-conscious Mind, is there any reason I shouldn't make these changes?** *... With this thought you imagine the days transforming into weeks... the weeks into months... Knowing if there is any reason you should not make these changes, your other-than-conscious mind will let you know in consciousness...*

With your body relaxing as your mind relaxes, the other-than-conscious can reveal what stops you from making these changes. Now you can ask, **Other-than-conscious Mind, can you begin a process of re-education that will retrain the past so that I can accept the bright and compelling future you hold for me?** *... Then let yourself go deeper and deeper still... Notice with each word that is uttered, each breath that you take, that you are staying in that relaxed, comfortable state... a state of deep and profound relaxation.*

In this state of relaxation, the other-than-conscious mind will reveal your hidden talents and skills that will allow you to accomplish the goal you have in mind...Imagine how you will use these talents in the next day... in the next week... and then through the rest of your life.

Take in another deep, cleansing breath... letting it go with a sigh... from here, allow the other-than-conscious mind to show you the positive benefits of making this change... Imagine the people you will see... the conversations you will have... the discoveries that will convince you that working with your mind is no small thing… It is a big thing that can and will be done in a very easy way.

With this powerful force working with you, ask inside, Other-than-conscious Mind, is there any part of me, conscious or unconscious, that disagrees with the changes upon awakening?…

If there are no disagreeing parts ask, Other-than conscious Mind, would you be willing to use these changes to help me accomplish my goals safely and quickly?…

If there is a part that objects… please thank that part of you for being there… Thank it for being there and ensuring the integrity of your mind… And ask that part if over time it would agree to use the new behaviors once they are proven to work upon awakening….

With 100% agreement now, what is the other-than-conscious going to do upon awakening to convince you that every day in every way you are going to get better… Allow your mind to drift through time… allowing the seconds to expand into minutes… minutes into hours… hours into days… noticing the changes one day at a time that will convince you that your mind is working with you… At this time, I want you to thank your other-than-conscious for being there… It is there beating your heart… it is there helping you to breathe… From here imagine once again going on a mental vacation… perhaps a trip to the ocean… or maybe to the woods… It's totally up to you… I want you to take all the time you need… And when you have spent all the time you need I want you to count yourself back to fully awakened consciousness…. 1, become aware of the room that you are in… 2, focus on the feeling of your clothes against your skin… 3, noticing each time you are going deeper and deeper… 4, with a perfect memory and recall of all that the other-than-conscious has shared… 5, eyes open, wide awake, feeling fine and in perfect health… And this is so.

OUTCOME QUESTIONS

As you read over these ten questions, think about how each might be restated to become outcome questions you can ask your clients. Consider how you might use these questions for a client who wishes to stop smoking, or lose weight, or conquer a fear. Please take some time to answer the questions for yourself:

1. What would you like to attain from Psycho-Linguistics?

    _____

    _____

    _____

2. When would you like to have these changes?

    _____

    _____

    _____

3. How often will you need to display these behaviors to convince you that you have made a change?

    _____

    _____

    _____

4. Is there any reason you shouldn't make this change?

    _____

    _____

    _____

5. What stops you from making this change on your own?

_____

_____

_____

6. Have you ever made a similar change?

_____

_____

_____

7. What are the positive benefits of making this change?

_____

_____

_____

8. Is there any part of you that doesn't want the change?

_____

_____

_____

9. Is there any place you don't want the change?

_____

_____

_____

10. **What will need to occur during the process for you to make the change?**

_____

_____

_____

Note that, as the hypnotist, you must be convinced you have all the necessary information to guide your client to a successful change.

Notice that the above questions all begin with: **What? Where? How? When? With Whom?** Because it is so essential for success, I reiterate here, the word _"why"_ should be eliminated from any therapeutic session. You will find it nowhere in this list or any of the patterns of Psycho-Linguistics. The reason _"why"_ has nothing to do with any change, and will in no way move that person toward success in the future.

On the other hand, if you elicit how success will be accomplished, when it will occur and with whom... you are setting up the mind's process for success. If you focus on success, your chances of achieving success are much greater.

WHAT ARE IMPACT WORDS?

Do you recall how, as you grew out of childhood and into adolescence, you developed that one special friendship or a close knit group of friends? Chances are that your circle of friends developed an exclusive language code involving words and phrases that were unique to the members of that circle. These words began to develop a special meaning for you and began to have a certain _impact_ on your consciousness.

Through life's experiences, we all progressively develop a structure of belief. Within this belief system there are certain words that have a special meaning for us. My impact words are most likely very different from yours, and yours are very different from your neighbor. Impact words are an individual's own set of words that will have the greatest impact on his or her consciousness.

There are questions that will elicit the client's impact words and help to ensure the safe fulfillment of his or her outcomes while keeping in mind the proper balance or ecology.

Take a moment and answer the following four questions. If you need more room, please use a piece of note paper.

1. **What has to be present in a job for you to enjoy it?**

   _____

   _____

   _____

   You will soon be putting your client's mind to "work." In order to do it successfully, you must know what the individual's underlying positive motivation is and how it works. Then, during the session, you can tap into a pre-existing motivation strategy by using the motivating impact words. All suggestions and programming techniques can be structured with the use of impact words so they make sense to, and have an impact on, the person receiving the programming.

2. **What has to be present in a relationship for you to enjoy it?**

   _____

   _____

   _____

   The importance of asking about relationships is simple. When the behavior changes are made, your client will have a new relationship with his or her inner self. For the new programs to feel right, they must be stored with the positive relationship programs of the past. By using the relationship impact words within the suggestions, it will allow the new programs the respect needed to be accessed and used.

3. What has to be present in a hobby for you to enjoy it?

_____

_____

_____

Your client has come to you because he or she wants the new programs to be easy and accomplished with a minimal effort. How easy is it to accomplish a task when it feels as if you are doing something you enjoy? The client is not only using the new program, but is enjoying using it as well!

4. How do you know when you have done a good job?

_____

_____

_____

Most people will have some method of judging information; whether it is good, bad or indifferent. By gathering this information you can set up the suggestions to move along a timeline of success with which the individual is comfortable. In other words, because this person must be capable of believing that success is possible, you are setting up guidelines within his or her belief structure. The response to this question will also let you know whether your client uses internal or external processing to accept information. Which means, does this individual know from within that he or she is doing well, or does this acceptance need to come from someone else?

Impact words hold a special meaning for a particular person. Because impact words have a direct impact on the psyche of the client, they are used in every session to instill a deep level of trust and rapport. You will also find that impact words are the basis for the modeling process. This is the process of watching someone demonstrate a behavior and learning from the internal and external cues how to imitate that behavior so you can get the same result. The patterns of Psycho-

Linguistics were modeled from a group of innovative researchers in the fields of hypnosis, NLP and psychology. These are people who spent their entire careers modeling the people around the world who excel at their profession. With Psycho-Linguistics, you are taking their discoveries of success and motivation into the life of your client.

WHAT IS ECOLOGY?

Webster's defines Ecology as *"a science concerning the interaction of organisms and their environment."* For the purpose of therapy, we will define Ecology as the science concerning the interaction between the thinking process and its environment; the environment representing the total well-being of the person. If this person makes this change, will there be an increasing or lessening effect on the self-image? Is anything going to be lost by making this change?

When making changes, you must look at the ecology to make sure the modifications are upgrades in consciousness; an improvement in every aspect of the individual's life.

Within all change technology, there is no more important factor than that the shift takes place at the right time and at the right pace. This is one of the basic principles of Psycho-Linguistics; always look at all the angles.

1. If this change happens, are there any negative or less than positive side effects?

   _____

   _____

   _____

2. When this change happens, will you need any further training to keep you from harm?

   _____

   _____

   _____

3.   Are there any special precautions that you should take now that this change has been made?

_____

_____

_____

These are questions that would bring any ecology questions to the surface. As the answers are given, you can use your creative mind to guide the individual through the process.

As an example, if you want to help someone overcome a fear of water, you would want that person to first agree to attend swimming lessons before testing the results of the hypnosis. For someone who has no swimming ability, the fear of water is well founded. The point is to plan success on all levels so that there are no miscommunications. Always look at every angle.

HOW DO YOU DEVELOP YOUR HYPNOTIC MIND?

As you learn to access your hypnotic mind, it may seem as if you have more power than others. The truth is that, in a sense, this power is real. As a well-trained hypnotist, you have an *ability,* persuasive in nature, and there is a *response* that goes along with it – *responsibility.* The more you generate powerful and positive patterns for others, the more powerful and positive you will become. Your life will begin to flow in harmony. It will change in inexplicable ways and become enhanced. People will seek you out for counsel and for speaking engagements.

First and foremost, however, you must understand the laws of the hypnotic mind. *Transference* is a common occurrence in this world; such as the transference of responsibility for oneself from an employee to the boss or from a patient to the doctor. All transference needs to be superimposed.

I look at transference as an opportunity to shift disempowerment to empowerment by building a bright and compelling future for the client. I am continually building a future in which my clients, each and every one of them, can look out of their window in the morning and say, "Aah, it's a beautiful day, I know it's a perfect day for me to be successful!" Whether they know this consciously or unconsciously is irrelevant. The most important thing to know is that they are now becoming addicted to the world and to the life they have chosen to live – a life of abundance and expectancy, filled with positive changes – for change is truly the nature of all things.

So now you know, the real control is in *allowing* the other-than-conscious mind to do what it does best. There is a power that is far superior to the conscious mind and it is the job of the hypnotist to prove that this power exists. It has always been there for each client who has walked through the doors of a hypnotist's office. Most people will be unaware that they have ever entered into the hypnotic state, but they will see, hear and experience the changes upon awakening.

The element of control is in helping your client to recognize that part which has always been there inside, but that he or she has thus far been unable to experience in life. You are going to prove that this greater part exists and that within it lies success.

"People hate me because I am
a multifaceted, talented, wealthy,
internationally famous genius."

JERRY LEWIS

Chapter Five

Techniques for Altered States

Placing a person in an altered state can be done through any number of techniques. Watch a good salesman sometime. He has Mrs. Buyer driving that car or trying out that vacuum cleaner before she knows what hit her. She was put into an altered state, without ever knowing it happened.

Any technique used with a person to either test or gather information involves placing that individual into an altered state. The purpose of this chapter is to give you tangible and usable techniques to guide yourself or another person into the altered state of hypnosis.

The ensuing chapters will cover a variety of techniques, but this is in no way the limit of approaches that the trained hypnotist has at his or her disposal. For each hypnotist, there are no limitations. The Psycho-Linguistics techniques are designed to work in a non-contextual format. They can work for any area of change or enhancement desired. These methods can be interwoven, one with another. I never limit a client's success by restricting the session to one method or technique. I believe that, for each individual, there is a tapestry for change… it is my job to weave together each client's new concept of reality.

WHAT IS THE EYE ROLL TRANCE TECHNIQUE?

Although the Eye Roll Trance is usually a part of the testing process, it can also be used for integrating a selective state. Therefore, this method is included as part of this section.

First have the subject roll the eyes upward. Place your finger on the forehead at the hairline to give the subject a focal point.

Eye Roll Script:

Keeping your eyes focused on the spot where my finger touches your forehead, roll your eyelids down... imagine that the muscles and tendons around the eyes are going loose, limp and completely relaxed... relax them to the point where they won't open at all. When you realize that they could open, but you are imagining that they won't open at all... just try to open them...

Notice that it's just too much work... and stop trying... there is no reason for you to try anything... you follow along with my voice and you relax... you are learning to use your mind... for a purpose... today it is to remove stress from your body...

Let all body parts relax by allowing a wave of relaxation to start from your facial muscles and tendons, and let it flow down through your body, through the scalp and to the neck, down to the shoulders and arms all the way to the tips of the fingers. Relax...

You are learning to let go... each time that you roll your eyes up with the intention of going into hypnosis, you find yourself going deeper... further inside... becoming less and less aware of your surroundings and becoming more and more aware of your powerful mind...

From here, notice your level of relaxation... and go deeper... and deeper still... become aware of the feeling of relaxation in the chest, abdomen and back, allowing all inner organs to go loose, limp and totally relaxed... negative thoughts, negative attitudes and negative beliefs will have no control of you at this or any of the other levels of consciousness... You will always remain in complete control.

Notice the level of relaxation you are currently experiencing... This is but one level of relaxation; there is a still deeper level... At that deeper level, if there is a problem in your life, you will dream of its solution... just let yourself go... Feel the relaxation moving through the hips, thighs and knees, and, out the bottom of the feet...

From here I want you to imagine going even deeper... my voice is going to pause. When my voice returns, it will seem as if an hour of hypnotic time will have occurred... (Pause for 20 seconds.)

Each time you close your eyes with the intention of going into hypnosis, you will find yourself going deeper... gaining greater benefit from this relaxed natural state on the threshold of sleep... Its time NOW to return back into the room... I want you to take all the time you need... And when you are ready to experience balance in your life... your eyes will open... you will be in that moment... wide awake... wide awake... feeling fine and in perfect health... and this is so.

WHAT IS THE PROGRESSIVE RELAXATION TECHNIQUE?

This technique is generally used with people who take inferred suggestion or are so stressed out that they can't let go and relax. These are usually people who have never experienced conscious relaxation. This script will help you guide them into a natural state of awakened sleep.

Progressive Relaxation Script:

I'm going to ask you to close your eyes... and begin to feel the muscles and tendons around your eyes. Use your mind to make them tighter and tighter... and as they get tighter and tighter, just tighten them so tight with your mind and with your physical body... and then just let them go.

Allow a wave of relaxation to move from your eye muscles and tendons down through your body. Become aware of the scalp now... and use your mind and your body to tighten up your entire face, your scalp and your neck. Tighten them as much as possible… tighter and tighter now… and then hold it… hold on to all the tension of the day… hold on to all frustration… hold on to all anxiety… and with your muscles tight, take in as much air as you can… and now let it all out… let out all of the tightness. Allow the tightness within the scalp, the facial muscles and tendons, and the eyes to let go. Let the body fall loose, limp and relaxed. Imagine a handful of rubber bands… see them loose and limp in your hand… and now imagine your muscles and tendons that loose, limp and completely relaxed… just like a handful of rubber bands.

It is from here that I want you to move your awareness to your hands. Allow your hands to grip into a fist… making your hands tighter and tighter… hold on to all frustration for a moment… and then just let your hands go, dropping them loose, limp and completely relaxed. Allow a wave of gentle relaxation to move freely from the very tips of your fingers up and through the body… allowing you to feel a passive state of relaxation… knowing that each and every time you use this procedure, you are going to go deeper and further into the state of relaxation.

It is from here that I want you to once again grip down with your fists and make them tighter and tighter… and allow the forearms to get tight… and the upper arms now… all the way to the shoulders… making them tighter and tighter. Think of all the things that might anger you. I want you to try to hold on to that anger… try to hold on… and then just let it all go… breathing out… letting go. Allow a gentle wave to massage all muscles, all tendons and all nerve endings… as you begin to feel a new feeling… perhaps a tingling sensation in your hands… a lightness or heaviness. Whatever it is that you are feeling it is uniquely yours. No two people feel the same in a state of relaxation. Allow yourself to go deeper and further with each and every breath you take.

Move your awareness to the bottom of your feet. From the bottom of your feet begin to tighten all the muscles within the feet and ankles… tighten all the muscles within the calves and shins… tighten all the muscles within the knees and thighs… all the way to the hips and buttocks. Tighten them now… tighter and tighter… and hold for the mental count of three… two… one… let them go now… breathing out… just let them go. Feel the wave of relaxation now moving into your body. Your physical body is now learning about the power of relaxation. It's learning to relax completely and deeply with the sound of my voice and through the power of your own mind.

So, now tighten once again, starting with the hands, the feet and the top of the head… tighten all the muscles from the hands, the arms, the shoulders, the feet, the calves, all the way up through the knees, the thighs, the buttocks, the head area… allow that tightness to move into the chest… and feel the chest and abdomen muscles tightening… the back muscles tightening… tighten every muscle in the body and hold it to the mental count of three… two… one… take a deep breath now… hold it… hold it… and now just breathe it out… let it go. Let it go and feel the body sinking into a state of relaxation… a state of deep and total body relaxation.

Your body is going to learn to go deeper as we go through this process one more time. When I ask you to tighten the muscles, tighten them even tighter than before. Starting with the hands, the feet, the scalp, feel the body begin to tighten all muscles, all tendons, all nerve endings… tighten all muscles in the abdomen, chest and back area. Begin to breathe in deeply now… tighter and tighter… and as you breathe in… hold on to that breath… counting now three… two… one… just let it out now, let it go.

As you let it go now, allow your body to sink into a deep rhythmic state. You're doing perfectly. You can now use your mind to scan your physical body to find any area that is still tight. Using your mind, imagine that all muscles, all tendons, all nerve endings in that area are going loose, limp and completely relaxed. You can now imagine that with each breath you are breathing in the word 'relaxation,' and you are breathing out 'all in harmony'… and now you are breathing in deeply the word 'peace'… and now… 'mental clarity'… and now 'mental calmness'…

Begin to think in your mind of a gentle pond. This pond is serene and peaceful and full of vegetation. The sun is just coming up, and across the pond there is a beautiful deer. The deer is going to the pond for a drink of water... and you're just sitting there... relaxing... watching it all. You can notice the birds flying... and the wonderful sounds they make as they communicate with each other.

As you relax here, you will find that your mind drifts off to a more beautiful place... it will be your perfect place of relaxation. My voice will now pause, and you will continue to go deeper and deeper into relaxation... In fact, the deeper you go, the better you will feel upon awakening. So, each and every time you use this technique, you are going to feel better and better about yourself. Each and every time you use this technique, your ability to relax the muscles and tendons of your body will come to you more easily and in a more progressive fashion.

Soon, and very soon indeed, you will simply close your eyes with the intention or idea of going into relaxation, and instantly, automatically, without a conscious thought, your body will mirror this state of relaxation and, in fact, take you even deeper. Deeper and deeper each and every time with more and more positive benefits upon awakening. The positive benefits will increase and intensify into your life making positive, bright and compelling changes to your future... changes that you will be willing to take part in upon awakening. My voice will now pause... (2-3 minutes)...

As you become aware of my voice once again, I want you to become aware of the state of your body's relaxation at this time... for you are going to carry this relaxation into your life. So begin to think about where you would want relaxation or the ability to be calm and at peace with yourself. Begin to think of the next day... the next week... and the next month to come. For soon, the days will become weeks... and the weeks will become months and the months will become years. Soon you will be thinking back over time, recognizing all the changes you made... changes that were instantaneous and automatic... relaxing and progressive... through the rest of your life.

It is from here that I am going to count from one to five... At the count of five, your eyes will open and you will become wide awake, feeling fine and in perfect health, feeling better than ever before... as if you have just received a deep peaceful and rhythmic sleep. From this perfect place of relaxation you will return to your life with a positive mental attitude about yourself, your world, and your ability to relax in the future.

One… hearing the sounds around you more fully. Two… allowing the blood to flow freely, with warmth of circulation. Three… personality in tact… perfect and powerful in every way. Four… with a perfect memory and recall of all that you saw, heard and experienced so that you can benefit from all the creativity. And, Five… eyes open, wide awake and in perfect health… knowing that every day, in every way you are getting better, better and better… and this is so.

WHAT IS THE SAFE PLACE TECHNIQUE?

The Safe Place Technique is designed to help your clients feel they are in a safe place where positive changes can take place. The subject is guided to a safe haven where hidden blocks within their consciousness can be uncovered. These blocks might otherwise prevent the subject from utilizing the hypnotic suggestions or their mental potential to its fullest.

I have also arranged this technique so that the hypnotist can use it in accessing the *hypnotic mind*. If, as the hypnotist, you are reading the script for your own growth and advancement, simply add in the sections divided with [ ].

Safe Place Script:

Just close your eyes now… and with your eyes closed, imagine the eye muscles and tendons going completely relaxed. Just take a deep breath in, and as you breathe in deeply begin to imagine the eye muscles going loose, limp and relaxed. As you breathe out with a sigh, let all of the tension of the day out… just let it all go now.

Because you have already been through the hypnotic processes many times before, you're going to find that your other-than-conscious mind has already begun the process of relaxation... so focus your attention and awareness on the powerful flow of relaxation. Become aware of your hands and feet and allow them to go loose, limp and completely and totally relaxed... just let go... let yourself go.

Become aware of the powerful flow of relaxation as it enters your arms and legs... become aware of the physical body and its relaxation... for the deeper you relax, the more benefit you will receive... and the more benefit you receive, the deeper you will go. Allow this flow and powerful feeling of relaxation to flow into the torso... into the buttocks... the pelvic area... up into the chest and abdomen. Allow all inner organs... all inner systems... all cells... to go loose, to go limp and to go completely and totally relaxed... just let go. Become aware of the beating of your heart... rhythmic and natural. Become aware of your breathing... slow and rhythmic. Take this time to connect the breath... breathing in... and breathing out. Now you can allow that powerful flow of relaxation to move into the neck and head area. Your entire body is now more deeply relaxed than ever before.

Imagine that a crystalline white light is now coming down from the very center of the universe. Allow this brilliant white light to move down through the top of your head and into your heart. Allow it to now radiate out from the heart to the very tips of your fingers... to the very ends of your feet... and to the top of your head. Begin to imagine that you are creating a powerful magnetic aura around you... a powerfully strong magnetic aura that allows only that which is good to flow to you... and only that which is good to flow from you.

Your powerful mind can now allow you to float back in time. Imagine that you are going back in time to a place when you felt safe. Feeling safe may be an image in your mind... a picture of a place where you felt very safe. It could be a sound, a certain type of music, or someone's voice talking to you. Or, this safe place could simply be a feeling... a feeling coming from within you. Whatever this safe place is for you, allow yourself to move into it and let it grow within your body... simply imagine that every breath could allow it to grow and build *within you. Allow this safe place to become a part of your very existence right here and now. Through the power of your mind and imagination, this safe place is resonating around you as your magnetic aura. You are safe. [**In this safe place, you are able to use your hypnotic skills to help yourself and to help others. In fact, you will find that all you have ever seen, all that you ever heard and all that you have ever experienced is now acceptable and accessible to your mind. You will use it when you need it the most, whether it is with yourself or with a client in the future.**]*

Take this time to create your own unique safe place by breathing in as I count down from three to one. With each descending number just let that safe place resonate out and fill the room... three... two... one.

Imagine that with each and every breath the safe place is now growing and building... to fill your body, the room, and even the building that you are in. And it slowly begins to fill the city. Your safe place is growing so that wherever you go, you now know that you have access to your higher mind. From the city to the state... from the state to the country... from the country to the world... and now from the world to the solar system... and from the solar system to the universe... and now to the omni-verse. Allow your amazing mind... through the use of your imagination... to expand and explore... transmitting and receiving the higher thought of your own being.

My voice will now pause and as I pause the seconds will become hours, the hours will become days and the days will become weeks. It is here that whatever change you may be working on, or whatever you want to accomplish today will happen. When my voice returns it will not startle you at all. In fact it will place you into a deeper and more relaxed place in consciousness... and this is so. (Pause for one minute.)

As you once again become aware of my voice, you realize that you will bring this safe place back with you... back from the omni-verse... into the universe... into this solar system... into this world... into this country... into this state... into this city... into this building... into this body... and begin to breathe energy into your body as I count from one to five. At the count of five your eyes will open and you will become wide awake, feeling fine and in perfect health, feeling better than ever before… as I count… one, coming back into the room… two, feeling the energy pouring through you with each and every breath, revitalizing every cell, every system and every organ… three, feeling better and better about yourself [and about your skills as a hypnotist]… four, becoming more and more positive about information as you have read or experienced it… and, five, eyes open, wide awake, feeling fine and in perfect health, feeling better than ever before… as if you have just received a deep, peaceful and relaxing sleep… and this is so.

These are the basic types of induction techniques and are a great starting point for guiding yourself or your clients into an altered state. It should be noted, however, that there are any variety of induction techniques, many of which will be integrated through the following processes. As you become more comfortable with the induction process, you may want to use your own creativity to develop methods for initiating an altered state. You will soon discover how easily the Psycho-Linguistics techniques can be mixed, matched, and individualized for any personality.

WHAT IS TRANCE MANAGEMENT?

So you have made it this far. You have someone in an altered state and deeply relaxed. Now what? For starters, when discussing trance management, it must be noted that very deep trance states of hypnosis are not necessary for change to occur. In most cases, it is better if the subject is in a light state of relaxation. Many readers may find this last statement surprising, especially those who have taken previous hypnotherapy training. Too often the goal of a hypnosis course is to teach you how to get the subject into the deepest trance state possible, and then rate your success on this basis. The hypnotic *state* is only a segment of an entire process, and is certainly not your only, or even primary, objective. The techniques that you will find in this chapter can be accomplished in either a deep or light trance state.

Less than 10% of the population is the responsive deep-trance type subject. If only deep-trance subjects were able to use hypnosis, every hypnotist would be out of business. In truth, almost anyone could get the highly suggestible type of subject to respond. Stage hypnosis, which is often difficult for people to understand, is a perfect example. Clearly the hypnotist is giving the suggestions, but it is the deep and very suggestible subjects who perform the incredible feats. This ability is known as *somnambulism*. People who demonstrate this ability are known as *somnambulistic*, which means "sleepwalker." These sleepwalkers are capable of feats that would otherwise be impossible or extremely difficult for anyone to perform. Full-body catalepsy is a good example. The body is made stiff and rigid as if it is an iron bar. It is then easily lifted and placed between the backs of two chairs. Some stage hypnotists have even been known to stand on the cataleptic subject or to break bricks placed on the torso of the stiff body. I do not recommend either of these methods as they can be dangerous, and are not necessary to prove the mind's ability.

Over the years I have met hundreds of hypnotists and hypnotherapists. Frankly, I am often amazed by the unusual and illogical approaches so many hypnotists believe are the way to achieve change. Somehow, the techniques of hypnosis have fallen short for many. Most seem to hope that if they can get a person into a deep altered state, that person will miraculously make a change. It is true that hypnosis is a "conviction phenomena," but simply getting the subject to an altered state certainly does not guarantee success in making a change.

The techniques to come are a synthesis of my experience with NLP, hypnosis, and a variety of other related methods. While learning and researching these techniques, I came to the conclusion that, in all trance sessions, it is important to establish a way of communicating with the subject once he or she is in the altered state. When using the patterns of Psycho-Linguistics, you are not going to randomly give suggestions to your subject. Rather, you are going to be putting him or her through processes that build unconscious patterns and lead to the desired life change.

WHAT IS THE NEGOTIATION FRAME?

When taking a client into the state of hypnosis, the hypnotist must be certain that the client is willing to make the changes he or she suggests during the altered state. Because speaking out loud can cause some subjects to awaken out of the hypnotic state, I have found it useful to set up the *negotiation frame*.

The negotiation frame is a safe and comfortable way for clients to communicate by using their index fingers and moving them slightly. This allows the client's conscious (aware) mind to track the changes that are happening at the other-than-conscious level of mind. The script below is assuming that you have already guided the client into the altered state.

Negotiation Frame Script:

Now that you are relaxed and comfortable... So that you know and I know that a wonderful change is going to happen today... I would like you to use the right index finger for "yes" by moving it slightly NOW... (After the client moves the right index finger continue...) You are doing perfectly... Take in a deep full breath... let it out with a sigh.

So that you know and I know that your powerful other-than-conscious is going to work with us today... Please use your left index finger by moving it slightly for a "no" response NOW... (Pause until you notice the response with the left index finger...) You are doing perfectly...

From this point forward, if I ask you a question, during this or any other hypnosis process, I want you to remember the right index finger for "yes" and the left index finger for "no"...

Now that you know and I know, you can relax and go even deeper... letting go of outside thoughts or activities... There is nothing that needs to be done... no place you need to be... This is your time to relax, let go...

WHAT IS UNCONSCIOUS RESPONSE?

After setting up conscious responses, you will begin to look for *unconscious response,* which will show up in a variety of forms. The client's body may suddenly jump, or fingers, legs, toes or the face may twitch.

Unconscious response often appears as movement concurrent with the conscious responses. When this happens you have access to the other-than-conscious mind and can assume you have congruity, or agreement, between the conscious and other-than-conscious. Once you receive a positive response, you use repetition of the positive suggestion to set in place the pattern for permanent change.

When unconscious response is contradictory to the conscious response, it is usually a signal of incongruity, or disagreement, between the conscious and other-than-conscious. As an example, you may see a conscious lifting of the right index finger, which is a 'yes' signal, but may, at the same time, see the left index finger or the left hand twitch slightly. At this point, one must assume that the other-than-conscious mind is identifying a part of the person that does not agree. When unconscious incongruity appears, negotiation with the other-than-conscious mind is in order.

Over the years I have found that receiving unconscious response is not quite as important as some NLP books would lead you to believe, but it is certainly a valuable tool for gauging your client's other-than-conscious congruity to a given suggestion.

Every client possesses the resources needed for change. If they didn't possess the ability to change, the desire for change would not be present. Most people simply react to life based on old, and usually inappropriate, programs. Many have built such powerful beliefs around the behaviors of the past; they now must seek the help of a hypnotist to access their own inner resources.

The negotiation technique is used in all the patterns to come and is the hypnotist's mode of communication during the hypnotic state. If there is a part of the client that is resistant to change, it must be handled with understanding. That part of the psyche has a legitimate reason for clinging to the past. It is doing the best it knows how with the information at hand. When the new, more appropriate information is presented, and the time is right for this change to be made, that part will be in full agreement. In fact, once that part discovers that the true underlying intention of the past can be met in more appropriate ways, the client will quickly begin to display the new behaviors and a new attitude. The mind is a success-motivated servomechanism. It will always make the best possible choice with the information at hand.

We all learn through repetition. Our minds work with the information of the past to produce our reactions in the present. By using the imagination, our minds are able to store into our brain the new patterns as if they were used often enough to become old dependable behaviors, thus changing the hierarchy of control to the new more appropriate behavior. The mind doesn't know the difference between real and imagined; it is all stored and categorized as information to be accessed and used.

WHAT IS IDEOMOTOR RESPONSE?

Similar to unconscious response, an *ideomotor response* is a class of unconscious body movement associated with the hypnotic state. Ideomotor movements are typically prompted by a hypnotist's suggestion. As an example, you may suggest to the client, *"Feel lightness in your hand, and allow your hand to gently lift into the air."*

As a hypnotist, you now watch closely for the ideomotor response to this suggestion. When the hand lifts upward, it is confirmation that your client has reached a responsive trance state.

Ideomotor responses are highly beneficial in building a communication link to the other-than-conscious mind. One may suggest, *"Your hand will return to your lap only as slowly as your other-than-conscious mind is willing to make all the changes necessary for you to meet your goal today."*

You will now watch the hand as it slowly (or quickly) returns to its resting position, all the while giving encouraging suggestions to the other-than-conscious mind. The movement of the hand is now a communication device between the client's other-than-conscious mind and the hypnotist.

Body catalepsy, or the stiffening of body parts without any perceptible conscious control, is another form of ideomotor response. Stage hypnotists sometimes demonstrate how parts of the body can be fully dissociated from the subject's conscious personality by creating body catalepsy in deep-trance, highly suggestible show participants.

WHAT ARE TRANCE MANAGEMENT METHODS?

This section is designed to give you some examples of ways in which you can maintain the altered state for your clients or yourself.

1. **Realize that everything you say has the potential to either deepen the trance or awaken the subject.**

   Example Suggestion: Everything I say and every breath you take will guide you deeper and deeper into hypnosis.

   All the information you gathered during the pre-talk is now your means of presenting the suggestions within your client's model of the world. If your client's lead system is *kinesthetic,* you are going to have to word your suggestions to let him *feel* them working in his life. This is true with *visual* and *auditory* access as well. The *visual* person will need to *see* the suggestions working and the *auditory* person will need to *hear* the new suggestions involved. In addition, you will use *impact words* whenever possible.

2. **Set up a blueprint of the session.**

   Example Suggestion: Whatever you need to see, hear or experience today, your other-than-conscious mind will create as reality.

   Remember to always go through the outcome questions before you put someone into the altered state. It is important that you know where you are going so you will know you are there when you arrive.

3. **Set up a safe place.**

   Example Suggestion: As you go deeper and deeper into relaxation, you will become more aware of your mind. Negative thoughts and influences will have no control over you at this or any of the other levels of consciousness.

Using impact words, and with the person's outcome in mind, you will find this very easy to accomplish.

4. **Give more than what your subject seeks.**

   Example Suggestion: If there is any cell, any system or any organ of your being that is not working in perfect order for you, then that system, that cell, that organ will now begin to function in light and in love, just as it was intended the moment when you were born.

   During any session, it is important that you point out to the client that the changes made today are stepping stones to an even better tomorrow.

5. **Give each client a reason to awaken each day.**

   Example Suggestion: Each day as you awaken, you begin to realize that it is the beginning of a new day… a bright new experience. You can begin to remember the moment you were born. You were given the opportunity of a lifetime with new eyes with which to see, new ears with which to hear and a body with which to function freely through life.

   Let your client's know that the moment of power is not in the past or the future, but NOW, and that as they take action in the present, their view of the past changes and acceptance of a better future becomes realized.

6. **Give clients positive statements when their body moves suddenly or makes unconscious response.**

   Example Suggestion: That's right… you are doing perfectly.

   Each of your suggestions should support the effort of the other-than-conscious mind. It is my belief that the conscious mind is like the laboratory or training ground for new behaviors. After the new behavior passes the test of the conscious mind, it is sent to the other-than-conscious mind where the new patterns are generated when needed. Take the time to pace the conscious mind into the acceptance of the more appropriate patterns and behaviors.

7. **Set up a testable process that will allow your subject to know that he or she is in a state of hypnosis.**

    Example Suggestion: Some people feel lightness or heaviness in their body; others feel a tingling sensation... whatever you are feeling is uniquely yours. No two people feel the same in a state of hypnosis... so move into that feeling and go deeper with each sound you hear around you.

    As stated earlier, in many ways hypnosis is a *conviction phenomenon*. Some form of proof must be presented so the person knows the changes are made. By following the process of Psycho-Linguistics, the client's mind accepts the changes without effort. Therefore, the client may have made the change and be totally unaware of it. You will want to instill this awareness so that the client can go out into day-to-day activities convinced that changes have indeed taken place.

8. **Build a strong and resourceful anchor.**

    Example Suggestion: Think of a time when you had the skills and abilities you now need for the future. Remember a time when you had confidence, pride in yourself and a positive attitude... breathe the way your breathing... see through those eyes, hear through those ears, sense and feel with that body...

    A resourceful anchor is your "ace in the hole." If you keep a resourceful anchor within reach, you can always guide the subject back to awakened consciousness in a positive state. It is important to guide your clients back to the fully awakened state seeing, feeling and hearing themselves as positive and motivated people.

The above suggestions are meant to be guides for you to follow as you develop your own style. Be aware of that style as you create your own trance management techniques. It is important to come from a point of caring, and let your intuition be your guide.

HAND LEVITATION DURING TRANCE TECHNIQUE

This technique is written as if the subject has already been placed into a relaxed state. We have found that this is one of the best techniques to prove to clients that they are in the hypnotic state.

Levitation Script:

Take three deep breaths... Notice how each breath guides you deeper than the breath before... Notice how well you are relaxing... I want you to become aware of your hands... become aware of the hand that is lighter... Notice that it is getting lighter and lighter still.

I am now going to give a direct suggestion to your other-than-conscious mind... Other-than-conscious Mind, you are going to make the hand which is lighter get lighter and lighter, but only as slowly as you can convince the conscious mind to relax the body... so the lighter the hand becomes, the deeper the body will go into relaxation... as the body relaxes the hand gets lighter and lighter still... each time that you practice this process, your ability to focus your mental energy on that hand will improve... Each time the hand will get light and lighter still...

That hand is getting lighter only as slowly as your other-than-conscious mind can convince your conscious mind to let go... Go with the flow.... For the lighter the hand becomes, the deeper you will go. From this point on, your hand will get lighter and lighter and begin to lift. It might start on your fingertips or perhaps your wrist. Just let it happen... (Repeat until the hand has lifted.)

Your other-than-conscious mind will begin to show you the future... a bright and compelling future... a future where you have all that you need when you need it most. It is a future filled with infinite possibility... After all, there are only an infinite number of possibilities from any one moment in time... Take all the time you need and slowly and progressively allow the hand to go down... only as slowly as you can believe and trust in a bright and compelling future.

You can begin to return back into the room, but only as slowly as you can awaken to look through new eyes, to hear through new ears, and to experience life in such a positive and powerful way that you will know that a change has occurred... and you can take a deep breath and return back into the room.

Hand levitation can be used in many different ways and is effective for letting the hypnotist know where the subject is within the trance state.

"The thing always happens
that you really believe in;
and the belief in a thing makes it happen."

FRANK LLOYD WRIGHT

"Courage is doing what you're afraid to do.
There can be no courage
unless you're scared."

EDDIE RICKENBACKER

Chapter Six

Disassociation Resource *Technique*

The purpose for the Disassociation Resource is twofold. First, most people seem to readily have answers to everyone else's problems, but are unable to find solutions to their own. With the Disassociation Resource, the client is able to look at his or her problem as if it is happening to someone else.

Secondly, when someone is in a "stuck" state or a negative state, he or she is not likely to make high quality decisions. Disassociating helps to move that person past the negative state and into at least a neutral state where a new perspective can inspire a fresh choice.

From the Psycho-Linguistics perspective, a disassociated state is defined as stepping away from, or not being associated in, a particular memory or experience.

To better understand a disassociated state, one most consider what it means to be in a fully associated state. When fully associated, one remembers or relives an experience as if it is really happening, with all senses involved. In other words, one sees, hears, feels, smells and tastes the experience fully. When an experience is happy or positive, full association is beneficial. However, for negative or traumatic experiences, full association can bring about fear, anxiety or even panic.

The Disassociated Resource allows one to view oneself from the perspective of an unbiased observer. As an example, one may imagine watching an experience on a screen from a comfortable seat in the back row of a theatre. From this perspective, the sights, sounds and emotions are on the screen, safely removed from oneself.

The ability to disassociate from a negative or traumatic experience is required before a new perspective can be gained, or a new choice can be made. Disassociation is reprogramming past events, building motivation and planning a new future.

There is one client in particular who comes to mind in regard to the Disassociation Resource. This middle-aged woman, named "Alice," came to me with a very troubled past. She was unable to recall anything of her life prior to the age of thirteen. She knew that something from her childhood was troubling her, it seemed each day of her life, but she feared her past so much, she avoided letting any childhood memories into her consciousness. Alice didn't know what caused such apprehension since it was completely hidden from her conscious awareness.

Relaxation was the first step for Alice to help her experience some relief from her anxiety. I guided her through a progressive relaxation and then began questioning her. Alice readily moved into a deep state of hypnosis. It seemed as if she was suddenly eager to resolve what had troubled her for so long. In this state, she began to relive the experience. Her voice tone and tempo changed and she became a thirteen-year-old girl again. Alice became distressed when she realized that something, she didn't know what, was about to happen.

I immediately had Alice become aware that she was in the room with me, relaxed and in a state of hypnosis, where she could easily review the scene in her mind. I told her it would be safe for her to go back to the time when she was thirteen, but this time as the adult she is today. I then took her a step further away by having her imagine that everything in that incident was, in fact, happening to someone else. Her other-than-conscious mind could now play out the scenario as if happening to another person and not to her.

Alice was now viewing the scene with very little agitation and the shocking truth was revealed. At the age of 13, an older neighborhood boy had molested Alice. This revelation brought many aspects of her behavior to light. Most notably, she now understood why she had always had a problem with men.

Alice was soon to be married for the third time. More than anything, she wanted this marriage to be different from the previous two. With a fresh perspective she began to see the pattern she had developed with all the men with whom she had been close. Once her relationships were established, she began to put up resistance and set up blocks to intimacy. Through the pattern of disassociation, Alice was finally able to reveal the cause of her disharmony in relationships. With her newfound awareness she could meet the men in her life on a new foundation. Every man was not this neighborhood boy, and they were not all out to hurt her.

When Alice first reviewed the event with the neighborhood boy, she described the situation with utter disbelief. Alice now needed to place that situation in proper perspective. I had her go through the experience again, knowing that she was in the embrace of a comfortable chair where she could safely make a mental review with the unique tool known as her mind. I instructed Alice that this incident could only be viewed from the mind of an adult, almost as if it were happening to someone else – only then was the other-than-conscious mind allowed to play out the true memory that had been hidden for so long.

Now, as an adult, Alice's past was set free. She began to recall other memories of her childhood – memories that were positive, bright and compelling. Amazingly, the one devastating experience had blocked her happy childhood memories, but now they were free to come into her conscious awareness. Once the incident was uncovered, it was as if a weight was lifted away. A radiant smile lit Alice's face.

Alice's initial reason for seeking me out was to shed 75 pounds of excess weight. Alice was thrilled to discover that she was no longer compelled to protect her body with excess weight. She was able to lift away the weight of the past by disassociating and unlocking the memories of her mind. If Alice had continued to try recalling the cause of the block without the Disassociation Resource, she may never have uncovered the true origin of her plight. Her mind would have instantly brought up the old fears and the safety shield that had protected her from the memory.

Although the Disassociation Resource seems very simple, I have found time and again that reviewing an event from a new perspective can unleash the personal potential of each client. In fact, I use this technique often as a tool for my own problem-solving.

Please keep in mind that the Disassociation Resource should be not confused with *dissociation,* which is a psychological process involving the disconnecting or separation of the elements of an experience, but not necessarily the changing of one's perspective, which is the key element to the Disassociation Resource.

HOW DO YOU GUIDE SOMEONE INTO THE DISASSOCIATION RESOURCE?

Disassociation Script:

Take a moment to settle back... You should be in a comfortable chair or lying in bed... With your eyes closed, take in a deep cleansing breath... let it go with a sigh...

Starting at the bottom of your feet, and working your way up to the top of your head, we are going to relax each part of the body.

Become aware of your feet... notice, by becoming aware of your feet, a sensation... a feeling of relaxation begins there... It could be lightness or heaviness... The feeling is uniquely yours... Allow that feeling to flow up into your ankles and shins... A feeling of no feeling, a sensation of no sensation... let go of the cares and concerns of your day... you are concentrating on the different parts of your body... As you imagine each part it goes loose, limp and completely relaxed...

Become aware of the feeling of relaxation as it moves into the knees and then the thighs, as the lower part of the body goes loose... limp... completely relaxed.

From here, shift your attention to the hands... Notice the tingling sensation at the tips of the fingers... Your hands are going loose, limp and completely relaxed... It is from here that I want you to use the right index finger for "yes" by moving it slightly... And the left index finger for "no."

So you can enter into the deepest possible state of hypnosis today give me a "yes" response... (When the subject lifts the right index finger, continue.) You are doing perfectly... Give me a "no" response... (After the response, continue.) Excellent... each time we work together, you will find it easy to respond to me using this "yes" and "no" signaling system...

Notice the relaxation continuing even as you concentrate on other things... Your arms and shoulders relax, and the chest, abdomen and back go loose... limp... completely relaxed.

Become aware of the current of relaxation that is moving from the tips of the toes and the ends of the fingers... The feeling of relaxation is flowing through the arms and the legs... meeting in the torso of the body... moving up through the neck and into the head... across the scalp and down the forehead and jaw... and the jaw goes loose, limp, completely relaxed.

It is from here that you can use disassociation as a resource... You can use your creative mind to imagine that you are standing across the room... From over there you are watching yourself relax... And when you have imagined that, just give me a "yes" response using the right index finger... (Pause until you see the response). From that perspective, you can tell you are relaxed... And go deeper and deeper...

I want you to think of a situation where you could benefit from this disassociated perspective... It could be a past experience or a future thought... allow your mind to expand... When you have a time in mind, just give me a "yes" response. (Pause until you get a response.) Now that you have that time, imagine that you have the power to change it. If it's negative, allow your creative mind to change the experience... Imagine what you could have said, done or experienced... Let the negative memories be stored behind you in black and white... imagine the sound slowing down to a point that you can no longer hear it... place the images and pictures behind you... From that perspective, allow your higher mind to discover the lesson learned... Once you have the lesson learned, give me a "yes" response. (Pause until you get a response.)

With this positive life lesson in mind, move into a positive memory... one that is joyful and full of life... Imagine that you have the power to make it even better... Imagine Walt Disney himself is colorizing this dream... place your favorite music in the background... Now, step into it... be there, enjoying the moment... take that moment with you into a deeper state of hypnosis... I say to you now... negative thoughts, concepts and beliefs will have no control over you at this or any of the other states of consciousness... You are learning to use your mind and for a purpose... Today you are learning to use your mind to create a disassociated resource, one that will allow you to rise above any situation... And from that perspective, realize the truth of every experience...

So this will be so. I would like you to take all the time you need to return fully back into the room... When you are ready your eyes will open... you will be wide awake... feeling fine and in perfect health... and this is so.

Please Note: When **setting up "yes" and "no" responses.** You can do this in two ways, with either unconscious or conscious responses. The unconscious response is done outside the subject's awareness, such as an involuntary muscle movement or an unconscious twitch. The conscious response, which I personally recommend, is simply set up by telling the subject, as you lift the index finger on one hand, that this is to be used for a "yes," and, as you lift the other finger, state that this finger will be used for a "no." (*Reference Negotiation Steps earlier in this chapter.*)

OUTLINE FOR
DISASSOCIATION RESOURCE

1. Set up "yes" and "no" responses.

2. Ask the subject to imagine that he or she is across the room look-ing back at his or her body over here. Then place your hand on the anchor.

3. When the subject has this in mind, elicit a "yes" response.

4. Break the state by having the subject deepen the relaxation in the body.

5. Ask the subject to think of a situation wherein he or she could benefit from looking at a situation from a new perspective. Ask: Where can you apply the resource in your life?

6. When the situation is in mind have the subject give you a "yes" response as each step is completed.

7. Suggest that the subject can return back into the room only as slowly as he or she can be convinced that there are now new and attainable solutions to problematical situations.

8. Bring back to fully awakened consciousness.

"A simple truth:
It's impossible to be depressed
when you take action."

DR. ROBERT ANTHONY

Chapter Seven

The *Power* of the Past

The seminar in New York City was going as planned. I had requested a volunteer for a demonstration. I asked if any of the participants could think of a negative event that, when thought about, brings about negative feelings and emotions. A young, dark-haired woman in the second row raised her hand. As she walked to the stage, I noticed her stark attire. She was wearing an ankle-length black dress, black shoes with heavy heals and dark hose. While a woman in dark clothing is not an uncommon sight in New York City, it made this woman appear vulnerable and sad.

Her name was "Nell," and she was a native of Manhattan. I started by asking her, "When you remember the event, is it in color or black-and-white?"

"I don't see anything at all," she replied.

I was not surprised by Nell's response. When asked to access the memory, she never rolled her eyes up to the visual field where a picture would be found. Clearly Nell was not a visual processor.

I then suggested that she raise her eyes up and notice whether the memory is in color or black-and-white. She vehemently refused to do so and instantly fat tears sprang from her eyes and streamed down her cheeks. In that moment I knew that Nell would benefit from the Power the Past technique. Here was a young, attractive woman with all the potential in the world. The world should have been her oyster, yet she was choosing to give away her power to a single memory.

I asked, "Is that past memory serving you in some way?" She immediately told me that it was not serving her in any way that she could think of. I then asked, "Would you be willing to talk about the experience?"

She wiped her tears, shrugged, and replied, "I suppose so."

I encouraged her to tell me about the situation. She started slowly, and then the words tumbled out. She had gone jogging late at night in Central Park where she was accosted by a group of five men and raped. She described the intense feeling of being trapped with no way out. If another jogger hadn't heard her screaming, she was certain she would have been left for dead.

My mind immediately began racing. I had never before had a volunteer reveal an experience so brutal and traumatic in front of a large group. What had I gotten myself into?

"Were the perpetrators ever caught or convicted," I asked.

"No," she replied, "They were never found and that was four years ago."

"What has happened in your personal life since that day?" She indicated that she was a social worker and, prior to the rape, she had had a thriving practice. Her days were spent helping people to improve their lives. Since that day, however, her practice had dwindled to just a handful of patients. She rarely went out, never dated, no longer exercised, felt tired all the time and, generally, just let each day drift by. When Nell finished talking, her shoulders were slumped and her limp hair hung in her face. "I just can't stop thinking about it," she said.

Nell's behavior is a prime example of giving away one's power to the past.

"What do you think is worse," I asked her. "Being raped once or being raped over and over again for four long years?"

Her head shot up and she stared at me, eyes wide. "How can you ask such a question?" she said. "Neither is good, and the thought of being raped over and over again is terrible."

"Without your knowledge, Nell, that is exactly what your subconscious mind is doing. As long as you are unwilling to forgive, forget and move on, your subconscious mind must keep the memory alive."

Nell blinked at me and I could see the light of understanding behind her dark eyes. "Think of it this way," I said. "If you leave your lights on when you go on vacation, you will come home to a very high electric bill, possibly much higher than you expected, because you used up so much energy. Nell, you are using up so much energy on this one past experience, you don't have any energy left for your current life. It's as if you've left all the lights on and the air conditioning on full blast for four years. No wonder you're tired and your career is at a dead end."

Nell's head bobbed in agreement. I glanced at the faces in the group and noticed several other nodding heads.

"Do you always wear black clothing," I asked. "Yes," she replied. "I actually have a colorful wardrobe, but I never feel like wearing it."

It was now time for intervention. I asked her, "Would you be willing to consider the event as if it happened behind you, somewhere in your past?" She nodded. "How far back would you need it stored?"

"At least 200 feet," she said.

I now wanted to know if she was bringing that past event into the future. "That's fine," I told her. "As you remember the event now, are you in the event, or are you looking at yourself from a distance?"

"I've now put it behind me," she said.

"Is there silence, or is there sound?"

"I can hear the men joking and laughing." She said softly.

"What happens when you speed up those sounds so they get faster and faster as if you're turning up a record player and the speed is going so fast, you can no longer discern what's being said? Is that less intense or more intense for you?"

"Definitely much less intense," she answered.

"Now take a little break and look around the room."

While she gazed around the room, I addressed the audience to let them know that I was having Nell look around the room to bring about a break state. I then turned my attention back to Nell.

"Go ahead, Nell, and remember the event. How do you remember it now?"

"It feels much less intense," she answered, her face brightening.

"Nell, what do you think might happen if you were to take this memory and remove it from your everyday awareness," I asked.

"I really believe it would free me to use my energy toward accomplishing my goals."

"Would you be willing to start exercising again? Of course, no longer running at night, so this can never happen to you again." I was asking Nell an important ecology question. When dealing with people's past situations, find out if the changes you are making will bring about any negative response. In other words, is the negative impact of the change any greater than the negative impact of the distorted thinking?

"I would never run at night again," she agreed.

"While visiting New York, I've seen quite a few joggers out in the morning. It looks like a safe time to jog to me. Would you be willing to run in the daytime?"

She was pensive for a moment. "I can't believe I never thought of that myself. It's so simple. Why didn't I ever think of jogging during the day before?"

The most incredible thing happened in that moment. She actually saw herself jogging. Her smile was full and broad.

"What happened?"

For the first time in four years I could see myself physically strong and healthy. I thought about starting my day off with a good jog, and it felt great!"

"Was it in color?"

"Yes," she said. "It was in brilliant color."

"Does it have your favorite music in the background?"

"It does now," she laughed.

"Are you in the event jogging, or are you looking at yourself from a distance?"

"I'm now in the event and it feels wonderful to be out running again, she replied.

"So what's happening with the past event now?"

"Well, I really don't want to think about that now, but when I do, it's in black-and-white, there's no sound and it's still, like a photograph," she said.

"If you could go back and reclaim that time, what might be a more appropriate thing to do at that time of night?"

"I could be reading, watching a movie, hanging out with friends, anything but going out jogging in the evening."

"Let's pretend that's happened, just for a moment. How would your life be different?"

She was animated now as she described her thriving counseling practice, good health, energy, fun with friends, and a fulfilling romantic relationship.

"Is there any reason you can't accomplish those goals starting today?"

"No reason I can think of," she said, shaking her head.

"Now one more time, remember that past event," I said. As soon as I noticed her thinking about it, I added, "Now put it into a picture frame behind you. Immediately make the image still. Make it silent." I paused a moment and then said, "Now hang it in the hallway of your subconscious mind. As it's hanging there, write beneath it exactly what you learned from that experience."

After I did a break state, I asked her, "What are you going to do with all of this energy that is now free from the past?"

She answered with a broad grin, "First I'm going to use it to start running again. Then, I'm going to start putting together a marketing plan for my practice. I know I'm a great therapist, and I now feel this experience will make me even better at it."

I then took her through a light hypnotic session and ran the pattern through at the other-than-conscious level.

When Nell arrived on the second day of the seminar, it was as if a new person had enrolled in the class. She was wearing a flowing yellow dress with colorful sandals. Her hair was attractively styled and her makeup, no longer severe, was fresh and flattering. What everyone noticed most, however, was Nell's dazzling smile. I overheard several comments about Nell's transformation from other participants, especially those who had known her over the last four years. Everyone marveled at how one simple technique had made such a shift in this young woman's life.

WHAT ARE STEPS TO THE POWER OF THE PAST?

1. *Isolate the past event as something the subject no longer needs, wants or desires.*

2. *Ask the subject to communicate with you about the event. If it is in color, ask if it is less intense in black-and-white. If it has sound, ask the subject to change the sound so it goes faster or slower, louder or softer, and find out which one minimizes the event. If the subject is "in" the experience, recommend that the subject distort it, then categorize and organize the event by placing it 200 to 300 ft. behind him or her.*

3. *Find something with which the subject can replace the past event. You want to know what your subjects are going to do with their newfound energy. Are they going to use it to improve the quality of their lives? Digging up the past serves no purpose if it doesn't produce positive results in the present or future.*

4. *Have the subject access the past memory again. The moment the subject begins to communicate about it, ask him or her to change the color and sound in the experience. Make certain your subjects store the experience behind them in black-and-white, without sound, and are disassociated from the experience. Immediately ask the subject to experience the past event differently. Then ask the question, "What would life be like if that were to occur?"*

5. *Test the response. Be sure to ask your subjects to tell you about the past experience. If they haven't transformed the limited language, then run the power of the past pattern again. This time, put the images behind them in a picture frame. Have them write underneath the frame what they learned from the experience.*

6. *From here, you're going to future pace the result.*

Hypnotic Script for Power of the Past

Go ahead now and close your eyes. Take a deep breath and let it out with a sigh. From here, scan your body. If there's any tension in your body, let that part of your body go loose, comfortably limp, completely relaxed... so relaxed and comfortable that any outside sound, any outside influence, will simply cause you to go deeper and deeper inside.

The deeper you go, the more relaxed you become... The more relaxed you become, the easier it will be for you to reclaim the power of the past. When listening to this process, you will find it natural to accept, use and benefit from positive suggestions.

So this will be so, shift your attention from the hands and feet to the legs and arms. Let your legs and arms go loose and limp. From here, as your body continues to relax comfortably, your mind will drift back in time... drifting back to a time and place that was less than positive... and as you reach that less than positive place... that less than positive experience... you know that you are going to release it, and allow yourself to accept the best possible outcome from this process.

So as this memory comes into view, you notice that instantly you change it and it becomes black-and-white... After all, you practiced it once... and now doing it once again is easier than you ever dreamed possible.

Notice any sound within the experience, and that the sound actually speeds up... or slows down... or perhaps just fades away... so that now the sound is simply gone... It's as if you have stepped into a silent movie. Even the event seems to drift back through time... no longer a part of your present experience, but rather something that happened a long time ago to a much younger you. After all, you're drifting back in time with your current skill sets... with your current abilities... with all the resources you had before you ever closed your eyes.

With this new perspective, you can experience this past event differently. In fact, you will find it natural to forgive, forget and move on. If there is another person in this experience, you will find it's easy to forgive that person for not living up to your expectations... and it's natural for you to imagine that person forgiving you for not living up to their expectations of you.

As you release... as you allow and accept this past event, you start to think differently. You start to imagine how you can better use that past emotion... that past energy... that is now becoming motion... to improve the quality of your life upon awakening. You begin to think about how you use it today... how you use it tomorrow... how you use it next week... but most importantly, you're finding it easy to store, categorize and organize these past experiences as positive learning experiences.

Now I'm not sure exactly when this will all work for you... because your other-than-conscious mind is just getting started. There's a part of your mind that, each time you to listen to this Power of the Past technique, will release the past, enhance the present, and help you accomplish your future goals and dreams. It could have already happened... or it could be happening right now. It could happen next week... Only you know for sure.

So this will be so, what I'd like you to do is take a deep breath in, hold that breath for the mental count of three, and then let it out with a sigh. As you let go, I went you to drift back again to the point in time of that old outdated memory... and whatever would have to change about that event, allow that event to change now. Allow it to change in such a way that the past memory would be stored in black-and-white, there's no sound around it. In fact, take the experience and allow it to play 200 to 300 ft. behind you... gone from your mind, gone from your thoughts, gone from your awareness.

Each time you listen to this hypnotic process, you will find the experience becoming less and less intense for you until it's totally gone from your awareness. That may have already happened... or it might happen next week... It might be something you remember to forget a month from now. Each time you will find it easier to forgive, to forget and most importantly to move on.

So as you now imagine the other-than-conscious mind freeing up the past, it's easy for you to imagine a quiet clearing in a forest. This is your place... a special place that you can go to get away from it all... a place in nature. In this place, you're sitting comfortably on a log. You're now watching the wild animals of the forest from a safe distance. From that safe place, from the corner of your eye, you notice an eagle flying overhead. Imagine what the eagle might look like. What it's like to see in the way an eagle sees... as you now imagine yourself flying like the eagle, soaring amongst the clouds, and letting the wind catch your wings.

Just then, from the eagle's view, you see yourself sitting comfortably on a log and right there beside you is a present. You pick up the present… you embrace the present… you are totally caught up in the present. And as you focus on the present, you realize the past doesn't matter anymore. [Pause…]

Each time you close your eyes with the intention of going into hypnosis, you will find yourself going deeper… further inside… Finding greater and greater benefit… so that upon awakening you can take action and accomplish your everyday goals. Some of the goals you will set today… some of the goals you will set tomorrow… other goals will come to you next week… but most importantly, you are learning to release the past and remove all the blocks from your past… so you can embrace the present and experience the future fully, in each and every moment.

I'm going to count from one to five. As I count from one to five, you will feel an eagerness to awaken and embrace your everyday life. One… becoming aware of the room you are in. Two… you're becoming aware of outside sounds and influences. Three… you have a perfect memory and recall of all that you want to accomplish upon awakening. Four… every day and every way you're getting better, better, better and better than the day before. And… five… eyes open, wide awake, wide awake, feeling fine and in perfect health… better than ever before… and this is so.

OUTLINE FOR POWER OF THE PAST

1. Isolate the past event.

2. Ask the subject to communicate about the event.

3. Remove color.

4. Remove sound.

5. Move event 200 to 300 feet behind subject.

6. Ask the subject to think of a replacement for the past event.

7. *Have the subject access the past memory again. Have the subject change the color and sound in the experience and store the experience behind him or her in black-and-white, without sound, and disassociated from the experience.*

8. *Ask the question, "What would life be like if that were to occur?"*

9. *Test the response.*

10. *Future pace the result.*

"Shut out all of your past except that which will help you weather your tomorrows."

SIR WILLIAM OSLER (1849-1919)

"Events in the past may be roughly divided into those which probably never happened and those which do not matter."

WILLIAM RALPH INGE (1860-1954)

"Hanging on to resentment
is like letting someone you despise
live rent free in your head."

ANN LANDERS

Chapter Eight

Resource Organizer *Technique*

In the Power of the Past chapter, you learned a method of putting the past behind you in order to forgive, forget and move one. The Resource Organizer technique, on the other hand, is designed to use the power of the past to one's advantage, because that is exactly what everyone's past is – *powerful*.

Can you imagine what your life would be like if you didn't have your past to draw upon? Your mind would have to start from scratch every morning. It would create a new you, with new thoughts, attitudes and beliefs. At first glance, this may seem appealing – to awaken every morning with all your past blunders forgotten, but I assure you it would be far more harmful than beneficial. What if one morning you forgot all your morals when some jerk on the freeway cut you off?

Besides, the mind doesn't store events as they actually happened. Our memories store events based upon our *perception* at the time. Thus, we all change, delete, and distort our past. You will recall our two eye-witnesses to a single event with entirely different stories. These changes and distortions were probably not intentional, but, nonetheless, we are all guilty of this phenomenon.

The distortions occur because our *values* and *perceptions* play a big part in the way we store information. It is not the purpose of this technique to change anyone's value system, which is key to an individual's personality. The idea is to bring about a subtle shifting of perception over time as the appropriate behaviors bring about successful outcomes.

Using the Resource Organizer, the client will review the information of the past and organize it, then re-file it in a more appropriate way, thus bringing about the desired outcome.

The past becomes beneficial by virtue of thinking of it in a positive way. As an example, people become positively motivated once the memories of the past are stored in color with movement and sound.

So what happens if you have a negative time stored in Technicolor® and Dolby Sound®? The mind is positively motivated to bring more of the same events and experiences, which is ultimately negative.

In my experience, people who are the happy-go-lucky type, store negative memories in black and white, or behind them so far gone that they can't recall them at all. They remember good times in color, surrounding themselves with the emotion of that experience and with loving, positive sounds.

If the information of the past is stored appropriately – the good times bright and alive, the negative events stored out of reach – then only the positive times will be brought up in future situations, resulting in higher quality decisions and a better overall state of mind.

I once worked with a client for alcohol addiction. He was a salesman named "Ken." Ken had had an exemplary career, but something had drastically changed in the last year. Ken's sales had dropped off tremendously. Now Ken sat before me, his head and shoulders slumped forward, his hands wringing, as he described his problem.

A year earlier, Ken had experienced several successive failures, which were clouding his thinking. His usual motivation and determination were lost to him. Clearly, a whole new cycle had taken over. Ken developed a new pattern that involved getting up in the morning, methodically going through the motions, plotting out his day's activities, and as soon as he would receive a few "no" responses, he would discontinue his efforts, procrastinate, get himself a drink and swear that tomorrow would be better. He was swiftly progressing from a comfortable rut to a very uncomfortable one as pressure from his supervisor began to ensue and the effects of the alcohol took its toll.

Once Ken was in a relaxed state, I had him go back and review his memories of the past. By this point, Ken was incapable of accessing a positive and motivated feeling of success. Before Ken went on a sales call, he had already seen himself failing. The failure syndrome was playing continually in his mind; all he had to do was play it out.

I pointed out to Ken that his customers were probably quick in picking up his unconscious cues and nonverbal communication and that, although he was unaware of it, he was probably selling a "no" response. Ken completely lost track of what he had always known; there are people out there who need his product, and who want to buy it from him. He had always known that sales was a numbers game; he simply needed to knock on enough doors to get enough "no" responses to finally get to the "yes." Ken knew that in sales, "no" means "yes." He had forgotten how to look at the "no's" from this proper perspective. Ken was now looking at those "no's" as a colossal wall that would require a great deal of effort to climb. Soon the walls were so vast, and Ken was so tired, he didn't even notice when the "yes" response was within reach.

The first thing Ken needed was to change the way he was accessing information. I had Ken store every "no" behind him, as if it were money he was placing into his back pocket and ultimately taking him one step closer to a "yes."

I then took him through the process of mentally getting to "yes." I pointed out to Ken that what the mind views as mental practice, and what is actually done physically, are all stored together within the other-than-conscious mind. If each time Ken received a "no" response, he mentally experienced three or four *"yes"* responses, his attitude would change. The mind will take the median between the two and give him at least a neutral and positive attitude going into the next sale.

Although some people are simply not cut out for a sales career, Ken was, in fact, a superior salesperson. He had simply fallen into a rut of self-doubt through repetitive practice and an anchor, which he set mentally through his day-to-day activities; first by falling into a dull routine and then by failing to set goals and accomplish them.

As Ken began to review the memories of his past, I had him examine that year of his life from his internal timeline and reorganize it. Ken could now begin to view this time of his life as a learning experience.

He had experienced a year where he learned to fail; and he did it very well. In fact, he did it so well that he would never have to repeat it.

At the completion of Ken's sessions, he was able to go back to his career with the same attitude and enthusiasm that had brought him renowned success in his early years of sales.

With Ken's repeated practice of reorganizing his thoughts, he found himself on top of things once again, this time with an ace up his sleeve, because he was now trained to use his other-than-conscious mind to set up and accomplish goals. Ken was one again getting a high from success and, therefore, no longer needed or wanted alcohol.

As you read through the following technique to building a powerful past, remember that your past brought you to who you are today. So honor each and every experience, person, statement and dialogue that occurs within your mind. You can feel free to change anything to enhance the quality of your present day experience, because the past is only a memory, stored unconsciously, on the tapes of the mind. Only in the present moment can you take action to accomplish your goals.

There is no power in blaming others for where you are or what you are going through. The power lies in taking action and changing what you can. *If you continue to think what you have always thought, you will continue to get what you have always got.*

The Resource Organizer builds new thoughts about the past, which in turn create new opportunities for the future.

SCRIPT FOR RESOURCE ORGANIZER TECHNIQUE

Resource Organizer Script:

Relax by closing your eyes... Take in a deep breath and let yourself go... As I speak to your other-than-conscious mind, I would like your conscious mind to use the right index finger for "yes" and the left index finger for "no."

So you can relax and go deeper, just give me a "yes" response... (Pause and wait for the response, then continue.) Thank you... and feel yourself going deeper and deeper... So you know and I know that you will learn to organize your thoughts in a useful way, just give me a "no" response... (Pause until the client responds.) Excellent...

Notice your body's level of relaxation... become aware if relaxation comes to you as lightness or heaviness... let yourself go... From here I want you to journey back in time... back to a positive wonderful event... I am going to count from three down to one; at the count of one, you will be at that wonderful event...

Three... Feeling yourself journeying back through time... Two... Letting yourself go... One... be there now... Imagine you are seeing what you would be seeing... hearing what you would be hearing... Step into the experience... Be there now... When you have that give me a "yes" response... (When you see the response, continue by applying a tactile anchor to the back of the hand. You will hold this anchor until I suggest lifting it in the script.)

Fill yourself up with this feeling, like an empty glass container. With this full, wonderful feeling, I want you to move through time... Relax and imagine yourself moving through the memories of your past. Become aware of the good times of your life... stop and enjoy them for a moment... as you do, make the colors bright and brilliant in your mind... put all the love and emotion into each experience... feel free to put in even more love than you remember. Place your favorite music in the background... just as if a Hollywood producer is playing a sound track to your life...

If an unhappy or negative memory comes up for you, I would like you to take a snap shot of it... as if you are taking a picture with a black and white camera and the picture stops all the color, the sound is gone, and the emotion dissipates as you now place each of the images behind you... One by one place all the negative experiences of your past behind you...

When you have done this once, with the memories present within your mind today, just give me a "yes" response using the right index finger. And go deeper and deeper inside... (Pause until they give you the "yes" response.)

Now that you have been through this process once, you can easily go through it again. This time I want you to let me know when you are at the earliest unhappy or negative experience you can remember today. (Wait until you receive a "yes" response.)

Now place a large picture frame around that negative time... like one you would see in a museum... When you have done that let me know... (Wait for "yes" response.)

The picture at this time should be black and white. If not, simply imagine that it is changing to black and white... In fact, from here the picture becomes so light and so bright that the images are gone. You know that you had an experience in your past, but it is no longer within view. In fact, I want you to write on that blank canvas whatever you learned from the experience. That's right, I want you to imagine that you learned something positive from the experience of the past. No matter how terrible it may have seemed in your past, see it now and into the future as a positive learning experience that will, from this day on, help you avoid ever getting into a similar or worse situation in the future.

When you have completed that episode, move through the next experiences, recalling each positive experience... Take a moment and enjoy each positive experience... If any other negative experience comes up for you. You know exactly what to do with it now... Take a black and white snap shot of it and place it to the side... You will deal with those with the other-than-conscious mind... Once you have reviewed all memories in a useful, more productive way and you are once again back in this room, give me a "yes" response. (Pause until the client responds.)

Each time you use this Resource Organizer technique, you will find it more and more difficult to find the negative experiences... They are stored differently... They are stored as learning experiences... You know the truth... the past is a series of lessons and those negative experiences never need to be repeated again... You are focusing on the positive loving memories of the present as well as the future...

Begin asking yourself… How are these positive feelings going to benefit me in the future? Begin to see, hear and experience the future… all the positive changes that are going to occur for you in the next day, next week and next month to come… notice the benefits of changing the past…

Take a moment and review this process today… each time you find yourself thinking of the past, you will remember that you can organize the past… You can and will organize the past as a resource… You will discover the hidden lesson in every experience, allowing yourself to grow wiser and smarter each passing day…

I say to you now… negative thoughts, concepts and beliefs will have no control over you at any level of the mind… at this or any of the other levels of consciousness.

It is time to take a mental vacation. You can go wherever you would like to go, experience whatever would be enjoyable to you… When you again hear my voice, an hour of hypnotic time will have occurred… My voice will only place you in a deeper more peaceful place, knowing that each time you practice using the powerful techniques of Psycho-Linguistics, you go deeper and gain greater benefits than the time before… (Pause for 20 seconds.)

Only as slowly as you are willing to live in a powerful, positive state of consciousness do I want you to return to this room. Knowing that all you will need to do is think about the past and you will automatically go through this process, making all the changes that will enhance your life experience today… changing the way the past is stored so that, from this day forth, you are building a bright and compelling future. Take all the time you need to return back into this room… the seconds are like hours, the hours are like days and the days seem to be weeks… all the time you need to convince your conscious mind that the changes have been made will occur before you open your eyes … and this is so.

OUTLINE FOR
RESOURCE ORGANIZER

1. *Have the subject close his or her eyes, start the progressive relaxation and set up "yes" and "no" responses.*

2. *Get the subject to access a good feeling – set up a Full Sensory Anchor. (At that point set the tactile anchor.)*

3. *Guide the subject through time while holding the anchor.*

4. *When the subject comes to a negative experience, have him or her take a snap shot of it. Teach the subject to disassociate it and acknowledge the lesson learned.*

5. *Have the subject remember a series of positive experiences while moving forward in time. Suggest making them colorful with sound and then have the subject fully associate with the positive experiences.*

6. *Break the state, then reinforce the process with progressive relaxation.*

7. *When the client has completed this process, return to the past images. If needed, continue the above process until all negative experiences have been reorganized and stored in a positive way.*

8. *Once the changes have been made, guide the subject back through the relaxation of the body.*

9. *Then have the subject view the probable future with all the changes made.*

10. *Take the subject on a mental vacation and bring him or her back.*

"Don't go around saying
the world owes you a living.
The world owes you nothing;
it was here first."

MARK TWAIN

Chapter Nine

Compelling Future
Technique

The Compelling Future Technique is used in all situations, with all techniques, and in every hypnotic session. People come to see a hypnotist because they want their future to be better than their past. In order to have a better future, they must first clarify what, specifically, they want to be better. They must know when, the times or instances, they want it to be better. And, most importantly, they must imagine what that future will be like when it is better and all the changes are in place. With a clear outcome, they can readily create just how it will be achieved.

One of the fallacies of some therapeutic models is that if you talk about a problem, analyze it, label it and try to make sense out of it, somehow it will eventually go away. In my experience, analyzing a problem just gives you a "better problem." An understood problem may be more sophisticated, but it is a problem all the same.

The purpose of this technique is to program the future with the desired changes in place. We will use an NLP process known as *future pacing,* which means to mentally rehearse oneself living the desired future with the goal of creating behaviors and responses that feel natural and automatic. We will also use *post-hypnotic suggestions,* which involve setting up a program to be triggered by a future event, thus ensuring success.

Future pacing is achieved by having the subject access a desirable new future.

"What if the changes you wanted simply happened and you were in the future? What would you see, hear and experience that would convince you the change is made?"

A post-hypnotic suggestion involves linking the new behaviors and responses to a future event. Here is an excellent example of a post-hypnotic suggestion used for stopping smoking:

"Every time you see others smoking or smell the smoke of a cigarette, you will instantly know deep down that you are a non-smoker... You will see through the eyes, hear through the ears and sense and feel with the body of a non-smoker, a clean-air breather..."

Smokers who wish to quit tend to have the most trouble around other smokers. This post-hypnotic suggestion directly addresses the future experience of encountering another smoker, but with the resource of experiencing oneself as a non-smoker.

Post-hypnotic amnesia, uses suggestion to help a subject selectively delete or forget to access a behavior or the habitual link to a behavior. Post-hypnotic amnesia is highly beneficial in bringing about rapid changes to behavior. In the example of smoking, one might suggest:

"Upon awakening, you will remember to forget, by forgetting to remember, the cigarettes of the past..."

I've had the good fortune of working with a variety of people who have achieved great success in business and in their lives. In one such experience, I was working with a relatively successful millionaire in Scottsdale, Arizona, named "Frank."

Frank had a rather unique problem. He had made a million dollars three times in his life, but he was never able to hold on to the money.

While under hypnosis, Frank acknowledged the intense thrill he feels at the prospect of making a million dollars. Once the money was earned, however, the thrill was gone, so he promptly discovered the "thrill" of losing it. This particular millionaire had gone bankrupt three times and made a comeback each time. Frank heard about my unique process through a mutual friend and hoped that I could help remove whatever other-than-conscious block was preventing him from maintaining his wealth.

After a few minutes of discussion with Frank, I realized he was living out what is known as *a sabotaging belief system*. Frank was indeed building a compelling future, but it consisted only of making a million dollars. Making the money was the goal he had placed unconsciously in his mind. He would promptly go about making the million dollars, and then just as promptly lose it, so that he could again amass a million dollars. If Frank had been able to maintain that pace, he could have, in fact, been three million dollars richer, rather than once again building up his million.

At the time Frank contacted me, he had a business plan in the works that was on the verge of bringing him his next million. We began a process of "upping the ante" by building an awareness of his future; that it holds more than money and more than a series of life events. Frank could now lift the limits from his perception of the future. Investing that million and making it ten million, or even one hundred million, could achieve the same thrill he experienced from making the money.

Frank began to see his compelling future in a new light, one that would allow him to awaken each morning with excitement and a readiness to go out and get what he wants from life.

He realized that in the past, after making each million, he began to awaken each morning in a different way; he began to awaken with troubled thoughts about his money. He started making his investments with the fear of losing his money. He started making business decisions from a different foundation than the excitement that had brought about success. Frank was setting up his own failure.

Through the post-hypnotic suggestions in the Compelling Future Technique, Frank was able to set up other unconscious goals that could be met day to day. By creating post-hypnotic amnesia, Frank could remember to forget, by forgetting to remember, all past failure. He began to organize his thoughts differently, which changed his attitude. It was no longer the "million" he was going after, but it was a lifestyle; the ability to do all he wanted to do, as he wanted to do it. This lifestyle compelled him each day to awaken with motivation and confidence.

The Compelling Future will work for any type of life enhancement. Sports improvement is another especially notable example. One way in which an athlete will be held back from performing his or her very best is when a coach doesn't allow the opportunity for displaying talent and skill.

When I was a freshman in high school, I was what they call a "wanna-be" – I wanted to be something special, I just didn't know what.

I first decided I wanted to play football, but I would tell people that I was a "30-second wonder." With thirty seconds left in the game, I would run out onto the field, get into my position, give a growl for defense, only to watch the quarterback snap the ball and fall on it, while we would all turn and watch the clock… 30, 29, 28… down to zero. I would walk off the field and wonder why I had even bothered to go to practice that week.

As I reflect on that time, I realize what an impact my thought process had on my skill level. I had never even imagined myself in a starting position and I hadn't taken any action to improve my ability on the field. I slowly made a transition out of those thoughts. I began to run and work out everyday. I convinced my Dad that I just had to attend the University of Michigan's football camp, and so he let me earn the money to attend by painting the house that summer.

At the camp there was a coach who taught us about using the mind to achieve success. I remember his stories and suggestions clearly to this day. One day the coach brought in a place kicker to talk with the group about his success in football. This kicker held the record for the most consecutive place kicks in University of Michigan history. Here stood this great athlete before us, actually sharing his secrets to success. He said that before he ever kicked for an extra point, he would mentally see it going through the goal post and he would never lift his head to see if it went through until he knew that he had made the right connection.

Being the son of a hypnotist, I was entranced by what I was hearing. These athletes were using hypnosis! They were setting up a bright and compelling future for themselves – they were seeing themselves in the future, doing just what they wanted to do most.

The following year I attended another football camp. I had the opportunity to hear one of the greatest motivational speakers of our time – Bo Schembeckler. When Bo walked into the room everyone's ears perked and their eyes brightened as they listened to and watched this great leader. To this day I remember every detail of Bo leading us through a mental process of personal achievement. Whether he knew it or not, he was leading every one of us through a hypnotic process for goal programming. I remember later hearing the story of a lineman who, during the half-time of a football game, ran completely through the steel door that led to the playing field because he was so fired up and emotionally moved. He had just participated in one of Bo Schembeckler's half-time talks.

We can accomplish this same motivation within ourselves and, as hypnotists, help others to experience it as well. We simply need to know the right buttons to push, the appropriate future to perceive and the right words to say to ourselves or to others. Thoughts do indeed become actions, but it is a process. We must perceive a bright and compelling future before it can ever be achieved.

As you go through the steps to the Compelling Future, follow the mechanics of seeing, hearing and experiencing your future in the way you want it to play out. Then watch out and hold on – because your dreams will soon become reality. There is an adage that goes something like this: *"Life seems to go faster when you are living your dreams."* Become aware of the dreams that you are dreaming so you can live what you want to live when you awaken.

To use the technique, simply follow the steps below. These patterns are like templates for you to fill in with your own unique style and with the information that pertains to the individual client at hand. To be successful, each hypnotist must be willing to be flexible with these patterns.

STEPS TO CREATING A COMPELLING FUTURE

Compelling Future Script:

Your eyes should be comfortably closed... take in three deep, cleansing breaths... With each exhalation, watch yourself go deeper and deeper... each time that you close your eyes with the intention of going into hypnosis, you will find that it gets easier and easier to relax... So with just the thought of relaxation and the intention of relaxation, you will be ten times more relaxed than you are right now...

From here you will notice that with each word that is uttered, each breath that you take, you will relax and go deeper... You will find it easy to use the right index finger for "yes" and the left index finger for "no"... Each time moving the finger slightly and finding yourself going deeper and deeper...

Now that you know how to relax, imagine one of your goals... Once you have it in mind give me a "yes" response... (Wait for the response.)

With this goal in mind, imagine that it is accomplished... You have done it... Imagine what you see, hear and experience when stepping into that future goal? What is your breathing like when you have accomplished that goal? Become, for a moment in time, your future self. Take all the time you need and when you have done that give me a "yes" response... (Wait for the response.)

From here imagine moving backwards through time, from the future back to this moment in time... Notice in reverse each of the steps that help you accomplish that goal...And when you are aware of the first thing you will do upon awakening that will convince you, just give me a "yes" response... (Wait for the response.)

With the steps in mind, is there any reason you shouldn't accomplish that goal? (Look for the finger response. Be sure to also watch for unconscious response.)

Skip This Paragraph if the subject is in full agreement. Should you get a signal that there is a reason not to accomplish this goal, ask the following question: Would the part that is responsible for that reason be willing to consider accomplishing that goal if its positive intent was met in a healthy and positive way?... (Watch for the "yes" response. If you get a "no" at this point, start the process over from the top and ask the subject to think of a goal that is attainable and acceptable.)

Excellent... At this level of the mind there is 100% agreement in making the changes necessary so that you can accomplish your goals... Take in three deep cleansing breaths... (Wait until the subject has taken the breaths. During the last exhalation begin speaking.)

Each time you close your eyes with the intention of going into hypnosis, you will find yourself going deeper... deeper and deeper inside. Making that powerful connection so that each time you think of the future, you will concentrate on your bright and compelling future... before you return fully into the room... Step once again into the future... be there now... seeing what you will be seeing... hearing what you will be hearing... experiencing everything as if it has already happened... Spend a moment in time there enjoying the benefits of your own mind... (Pause for 10 seconds.)

From here return slowly back into the room... Only as slowly NOW as you can accept, use and benefit from the power of your own mind. Knowing that negative thoughts, concepts and beliefs will have no control over you at any level of the mind... at this or any of the awakening levels of consciousness... When the changes are locked in place, and you know you can and will accomplish your goals, you will be wide awake, feeling fine and in perfect health... And this is so.

OUTLINE FOR CREATING A COMPELLING FUTURE

1. Use a progressive relaxation technique and set up "yes" and "no" responses.

2. Once relaxed, ask the subject to think of a goal he or she would like to accomplish. Get a "yes" response and use submodalities (Visual/Auditory/Kinesthetic) to create a strong positive anchor.

3. Fully associate the subject into the experience. Is there any reason he or she shouldn't accomplish this goal? If there is, negotiate an agreement.

4. Have the subject review the steps that lead to the goal, but in reverse. Suggest that the subject notice what events took place so that this outcome could become reality as quickly as possible. Have the subject focus on the first step he or she will take after the session.

5. Break the state. You do this by increasing the relaxation in the body.

6. Have the subject once again move through the next day, next week, next month to come and then to the day when the goal has become a reality. Elicit a "yes" response when the subject has the day in mind, then re-anchor the state and bring the subject back into the room with positive feelings.

"They always say that time changes things, but you actually have to change them yourself."

ANDY WARHOL

Chapter Ten

Resource Generator *Technique*

Every individual has inherent talent, skills and abilities that serve to define their personality. The purpose of the *Resource Generator* is to take advantage of these unconscious gifts by placing them into desired situations where they can bring about profound positive changes and enhancements.

As discussed earlier, we create our perception of reality through our values, beliefs and past programming. We also tend to assume that what is true for one person is true for another, which is usually not the case at all.

We all personally define reality through our own senses. Therefore, we have every right to redefine our actions so they become powerful and positive, helping us to reach our goals on a day-to-day basis.

Another way to explain this was told by my good friend, Gil. He tells a story he calls The Three Umpires, and it goes something like this:

There was a runner well on his way from first to second base. The throw was close, but as he reached the plate, the umpire called him out. Another umpire, as he ran toward the plate, called the runner safe. And so the argument began. The home plate umpire watched this incident in silence and finally walked slowly out to second base to hear what was going on. After listening to the men in turn as they each argued their case, he promptly corrected them both, "You're both wrong," he said. "This man is neither out nor safe until I say he is!"

Thus is the story of life, it is neither good nor bad until you say it is.

Unfortunately, reality doesn't come with clear-cut definitions. We form our opinions and shape our destinies with the information at hand.

Consider what might happen if you were in a positive state of mind all the time. What could you motivate yourself to do if you could, without conscious effort, simply take action and accomplish your goals? What if how other people perceived the goal didn't matter at all – all that mattered was how you felt about its importance? If all this happened, wouldn't accomplishing your goals become a breeze?

I believe accomplishing goals can be this easy. The best rule of thumb is to start slowly and trust that success will stay with you all your life.

Nothing complements success better than the ability to change and modify old beliefs or outdated concepts. Be prepared to soar like the eagles or contemplate like the owls – whatever is necessary for success. Flexibility at a time of frustration makes you a person in demand.

During a personal training session with a hypnotist-intern named "Phillip," I asked him to think of something in particular that he wanted to work on in his life. Phillip immediately spoke up and said "motivation!" He explained, "It seems as if those things I really want to accomplish in life, I put off. Even when I know that if I do them I could be far more successful than before."

I told Phillip not to worry because most people are just like him. They know exactly what to do, but don't know how to do it, or are afraid to change their lives.

Phillip wanted to know why this is so when they know the change will make their lives better. The reality is they know, on some level, that once they make the change, they will be unable to return to their comfort zone – or what they now perceive as their comfort zone.

I explained to Philip that people would love to have some kind of internal generator to build resources for them, without any conscious effort, but they don't know how to do it. This is exactly what we are setting up with the Resource Generator technique. We activate the mind to work with the existing unconscious behaviors, but in new ways.

Phillip looked somewhat unconvinced, so I explained further. I told him that when he works with clients, he will need to take a moment before the session to figure out how to word his session for that individual's needs. What if he could begin to think of all clients as an extension of himself?

Since clients will come to him for help out of a conscious belief that he can help them, why not use that same belief to help himself?

When you are working in the realm of the mind, there is no reason you can't work on yourself at the same time. I explained how, while doing a session with a client, it has often helped me to think that I was actually working on an unconscious part of myself, a part of which I was unaware, until this person decided to pay me to *work on myself.* This one thought keeps me positive and motivated toward each new client. But, most importantly, it keeps me in a state of learning and understanding, and in tune with the hypnotic mind. This has helped me time and again when those inevitable moments of frustration overcome me – I can suddenly become flexible. If I could be as much like that person as possible, I could then ask myself, "What would I say to myself in this situation?" Invariably, I become able to deliver an unconscious dialogue that seems to fit his or her needs and beliefs.

I wouldn't say that this has worked 100% of the time, but it has certainly worked often enough to make it a useful tool that I use regularly. If you find yourself in a "stuck" state, always remember that when you have prepared yourself, something positive will come of it. The mind works with intention. As long as your intention is to help, the message will come across as healthy and positive.

As Phillip sat in on my sessions during that week, he realized that almost everyone, whether seeing me for insomnia, weight control, stopping alcohol or smoking, they all lacked sufficient motivation for inspiring the change. One day, toward the end of the week, Phillip said to me, "I guess you're right, most people do lack motivation."

I told Phillip he was almost right. In truth, these people didn't so much lack motivation, but they were missing the desired outcome. They did indeed express a motivation – *one toward the old behavior.* They lack motivation toward the new behavior because their other-than-conscious mind has not yet realized the benefits of the new behavior. The mind always draws from the past and makes decisions based on repetitive behavior.

When the mind is making a choice, it will go deep inside to identify the responses of the past. Then, using the average behavior, will feed out a response. When feeling on top of the world, you usually respond to negative situations better than if you are feeling down. However, if you were to place the information and the resource into a generative mode – which means to contact something inside of you that happens repeatedly and link it to the new response – it will become like a friendly old habit. When it is linked in a positive way, it will be like a resource "generator" because the stimulus is already present; all you need to do is generate the new behaviors. If this process is done consciously at first, it will become an unconscious behavior rather quickly, because the comfort of the old stimulus is built right in.

After learning the Resource Generator, and going through the process himself, Phillip's motivation began to transform. He had spent so much time motivated about procrastination that he became an expert at it. He was so motivated about putting things off, he had no motivation left to do what he really wanted. All Phillip needed was a change of focus and a shift in his thoughts. He could then be prepared to succeed! For Phillip, as for most people, it wasn't a matter of success or failure. Rather, it was a matter of *doing*.

As you read through the Resource Generator, always remember you are in power – it's your life, your world, and your day. So, today is a very wonderful day to make a change. It is the natural way of the universe.

"Everything in the Universe
is subject to change.
It is the nature of all things.
You are either going forward or backward;
nothing stays the same."

AUTHOR UNKNOWN

SCRIPT FOR BUILDING
THE RESOURCE GENERATOR

Resource Generator Script:

Settle back with your eyes comfortably closed... Take in a deep cleansing breath... let it go with a sigh... Notice that with each exhalation, you find yourself going deeper and deeper... Each time finding it easier to reach that perfect level of relaxation... that level where you can clearly see, hear and experience your hidden talents and skills...

Today you are using your mind for a purpose... The purpose is to build a resource generator... Your other-than-conscious mind has already categorized and organized all your skills... all your abilities... and will generate them in the appropriate places upon awakening... All you really need to do is follow along with my voice... Allow it to guide you into that perfect place of relaxation where you will become unaware of your body, but very aware of your mind...

It is your powerful mind that will build this incredible mechanism... unconscious and automatic... Each time you practice using these hidden talents, they will work more effectively...

As you scan your body, noticing your level of relaxation, I want you to remember the right index finger moves slightly for a "yes" response. And the left index finger for a "no" response... There is no reason for you to consciously respond in any other way...

Each time you respond, you will go deeper... allowing your body to let go while your mind continues to build your resource generator... When you are convinced that this is so, just give me a "yes" response... (Pause until you see the response.)

You are doing perfectly... So that you know and I know that your other-than-conscious mind will work out all the details and you can be more successful than you dreamed possible. Give me a "no" response... (Pause until you see the response.)

Perfect... Feel yourself letting go... Allow your mind to drift back through time, remembering behaviors you would like to demonstrate more often... Some memories could be the ability to eat appropriately... the ability to be assertive... the ability to make a sound business decision... the ability to be relaxed and comfortable... It can be any ability you want to possess... When you find one specific memory, give me a "yes" response using your right index finger... (Pause until you see the response.)

Excellent... You are doing perfectly... Step into the experience... See what you were seeing... hear what you were hearing... fill yourself up like an empty glass container... When you are full of that experience give me a "yes" response... (Prepare to use a tactile anchor on the back of the subject's nearest hand. When you see a "yes" signal, say the following statement while applying the anchor.)

Imagine this feeling... Imagine this clarity of thought... Imagine this skill in three places spontaneously in the future... Take all the time you need... When you have thought of those three times in the future give me a "yes" response. (Let go of the anchor and wait for the reply.)

Is there any part of you that objects to your using this resource in the future? (Wait for the response.)

If you receive a "No," skip this paragraph. *Would the objecting part be willing to help find a resource that would be as immediate and more appropriate so that you can accomplish your daily goals? (Ninety-nine percent of the time, they will agree at this point. If needed, suggest the following.) Each time you close your eyes and enter into hypnosis, you find it easy to work with your other-than-conscious mind and solutions to your everyday problems will come into your mind...]*

Perfect... From here you can start to generate new behaviors where and when you need them the most to accomplish your loftiest goals... Notice the level of relaxation you are currently experiencing... This is just one level of relaxation. There is an even deeper level... You can reach that level by reviewing this process once again differently... In this new way you only need to review your day… In the review, think of where and when you need a resource the most… As you think, imagine your other-than-conscious mind journeying back through time, remembering every skill, every ability… every resource… Then choose just the right skill or resource for that moment in time…

You are building a resource generator… each time your mind will find it easy to solve your everyday problems with solutions found in the past, present or future… From this moment forward you are no longer trapped by your conscious thoughts… You know the truth… The truth is, there are only an infinite number of choices from any one moment in time… Each time you close your eyes with the intention of going into hypnosis, your capacity to accept, use and benefit from hypnotic suggestions will get better… better, better and better every day in every way…

Scanning your body for your level of relaxation now… Imagine letting go of the thoughts of your body here and now and imagine yourself one year from now… You have done it… You have accomplished a goal you set for yourself… It was easier than you thought… As you think back over time you notice how your resource generator instantly, automatically assisted you with the right thought, the right action, the right belief… With this thought, I say to you now… negative thoughts and negative beliefs will have no control over you at any level of the mind, at this or any of the other levels of consciousness…

Imagine moving to the day when you are convinced that you have all the abilities you need to continue displaying the behaviors into the future. As you begin to accept all the changes, beneficial behaviors and a fresh, new attitude, you can begin to return your conscious awareness to the room. But only as slowly as your conscious and other-than-conscious mind can come to an agreement that the changes are positive, permanent and lasting through the rest of your life.

Take all the time you need, and when your conscious mind is willing to use the resources of the other-than-conscious mind on a day-to-day basis to improve the quality of your life, your eyes will open and you can return fully back into the room… wide awake and in perfect health.

As you begin to sense the benefits of this new resource, you can contemplate on the times in the future where it will work for you unconsciously and automatically... At times this new resource will help you in the morning as you look forward to a new day... a day full of successful events and a successful attitude. At other times this resource will be there during your midday, helping you to handle the situations of the day in a positive and beneficial way... and at other times it will be there in your evening, helping you to discover new ways to relax and enjoy your evening activities... finding yourself more relaxed around family and friends... But, most importantly, you will find a variety of new behaviors and attitudes when you need them the most... as you need them during your life experience... and this is so.

You can return back into the room only as slowly as you are convinced that the changes are made. And when this happens, your eyes will open, you will be wide awake... wide awake... with your resource generator working perfectly... And this is so.

OUTLINE FOR BUILDING THE RESOURCE GENERATOR

1. Start the progressive relaxation.

2. Set up "yes" and "no" responses.

3. Have the subject think of a behavior he or she would like to display more of the time. (Get a "yes" response.)

4. Have the subject remember a time when he or she displayed the desired behavior. (Get a "yes" response.)

5. Ask the subject to now change this feeling to a color and then imagine filling his or her body with it. When the subject acknowledges that he or she is full of this feeling, elicit a "yes" response. At that time, anchor the state with a tactile anchor.

6. Break the state by asking if there is any part that objects. (Negotiate an agreement.)

7. Ask the subject to now think of a time in the future when he or she would like the resource. When this is accessed, apply the tactile anchor, and then make it a complete sensory experience.

8. Take the behavior into the future.

9. Bring the behavior back into the subject's reality and then bring him or her back into the room.

10. Suggest that the resource will occur unconsciously where needed in the future and guide the subject back to awakened consciousness.

"First we form habits,
 then they form us.
 Conquer your bad habits,
 or they'll eventually conquer you."

DR. ROB GILBERT

Chapter Eleven

Unlimited Reality
Technique

The Unlimited Reality technique is used when the subject doesn't feel that he or she possesses the resources needed to accomplish the desired change or enhancement. Sports improvement and public speaking are two good examples.

It has often been said that we were all created equal. Well, if this was true, then we would all be the same and the world would be a thoroughly boring place in which to live.

NLP, in one sense, is a study of people, and just what successful people do differently and consistently to get results. The Unlimited Reality technique is the framework one uses for accessing the attitude, belief system or behavior of another person. Through the Unlimited Reality technique, one can gain the resources needed to attain the same or a better outcome for oneself.

Unlimited Reality is my favorite technique to use with golfers. I usually start the session with one key question: "Can you think of a professional athlete who possesses the skills and abilities you would like for yourself?"

People willing to pay a large sum to be hypnotized for improving their golf game know their sport well and usually have at least two or three names immediately in mind. These clients come in with a jump on the program. They have watched and studied these exceptional athletes so many times, they already have appropriate mental tapes running in their minds; they just don't know how to use them. The Unlimited Reality technique is an excellent way to access those memories. With this technique, the golfer in your chair can have a very real experience as the professional golfer he or she has watched on television. The next time your golfer views Tiger Woods on television, he or she will no longer be an armchair official, but will be able to get into the game and be on the course, swinging the club with Tiger.

Whether training in golf, football, basketball or another sport, your clients can learn micro-muscle movements through a simple imaginative process, just as a child learns to walk and talk.

The bread and butter of a hypnotherapy practice are the clients who wish to stop smoking. When smokers walk into a hypnotist's office, they have no idea *how* they will be nonsmokers.

I once worked with a subject named "Ellen," who had been smoking for over fifty years. Ellen was so convinced she had no way out of her smoking behavior, she began to feel trapped within it. She had fully embraced the societal belief that quitting smoking is grueling, that she has a physical addiction to nicotine, and that she will gain weight as soon as she stops lighting up.

I started Ellen's session by reminding her that she was not born with a cigarette in her hand and was not placed in the smoking section of the nursery. Everyone is born a nonsmoker; the natural human condition is smoke-free.

I reminded her that as a child she learned by watching the people around her. Somehow, as a child, her eyes began to see, her ears began to hear, and her body began to feel, based on what she was experiencing in the world around her. She would mimic sounds by listening intently and watching the source from which it came. She began to move her muscles just right so as to emulate that sound. I reminded her of how she learned to walk. I suggested that it may have happened something like this:

Ellen was lying in her crib one day when she began noticing that everyone around her was walking around on two legs, while she remained on her back or belly, or at best her hands and knees. After watching for a time, she decided that if everyone else was doing it, she probably could too. She began to pull herself up. At first she supported herself on the side of the crib. She soon found out that standing on her legs wasn't as easy as it looked. The people who moved through her life seemed to do it with such ease. When she grew curious enough, she would let go of the crib, but would invariably plop down on her seat. At times the consistent falling may have brought about an unconscious belief that she would never be able to do it.

But something overcame that belief. Something inside of her told her that what others around her could do, she could also do, without question or hesitation. Ellen began to imagine herself walking like all the people she had been watching. She started out with crawling so she could build the strength in her legs and hips. She built strength in her arms so later she could pull herself up next to a couch where she would feel the firm ground beneath her feet. Suddenly, after all her practice, the muscles would respond perfectly and she would take a step, and then two. In no time Ellen was walking with ease, just as she had seen all the people around her do. She now takes walking across a room for granted. It can be accomplished without conscious thought and no effort at all.

I asked Ellen if she ever noticed how a baby, once having learned to walk, rarely falls down again? She nodded her head acknowledging that she had three children of her own. From the day they took their first steps, all three had walked from that day on.

I told Ellen this is the case with most everything we learn to do in life. If Ellen could now tap into that learning resource within her mind, she could indeed learn to be a nonsmoker.

Ellen had tried to stop smoking on her own many times. I explained that as humans, whether infants or adults, we learn through failure. But a failure is never really a failure; it is only feedback. Our brain continues to feed us new information, upgrading that knowledge, until it works and we accept it as truth.

As I took Ellen through the Unlimited Reality technique, she was able to think of a non-smoker she admires and then imagine herself as that person. As she sat at her desk, she imagined herself as her boss, who found it very easy to walk through the office without a cigarette. In fact, her boss had been a nonsmoker for as long as Ellen had known her. She found out later that her boss had, in fact, stopped smoking several years earlier.

Ellen realized that nonsmokers do everything the same as smokers, except they don't have the hassle, worry, or unconscious fear that is the byproduct of cigarette smoking. She had lifted the burden of the past by activating the unlimited possibilities in her mind.

There is a part of every one of us that absorbs new information and ideas through the experiences of others – it is called curiosity. If you were curious enough about how someone does something you want to do, would you be willing to imagine yourself walking in the other person's shoes? If so, can you imagine it with detail, including what is being said, heard, and experienced? Can you notice what words are being spoken internally? Can you imagine the rhythm of that person's breathing.

This process of imaging every aspect of an experience is called *micro-modeling* and it is the foundation of the Unlimited Reality.

The Unlimited Reality technique is for people who have no conscious concept of how they will act or respond with the desired change in place. I have even been known to send people out to rent a particular movie and watch it as if they are the character in the film, simply to get the experience from a different perspective.

You may contrast this with the Disassociation Resource as an *associated resource,* because you are going to fully associate yourself with another person's life and experiences, taking it on as your own and remembering that the other-than-conscious mind stores all information as truth, usable for future beneficial results.

STEPS TO BUILDING AN UNLIMITED REALITY

Unlimited Reality Script:

Close your eyes and think of someone who has a skill or ability that you would like to develop... Take all the time you need... and when you have found such a person give me a "yes" response... (Wait for the "yes" response. This technique should never be used first, so your client should already be conditioned to respond to "yes" and 'no" responses. Note: For ease of reading and clarity, the balance of this script is written as if the person the client wishes to model is male.

I recommend asking the client, "Is this person a man?" If the answer is "yes," proceed as written. If the answer is "no," you will need to change the script to "she" accordingly.)

Excellent... Now that you have found a person with a skill or ability you would like to develop, I want you to follow behind him as if you are watching him from a distance... You can notice the look on his face, the movements of his body as if you are right behind him as he moves through his day displaying the behaviors you desire... Take all the time you need... The seconds are like hours and the hours become days... and when he has completed the day displaying the behavior or attitude you desire give me a "yes" response... [Wait for the response.]

Perfect... Now, move through that day once again but this time imagine you are seeing through his eyes, hearing through his ears and feeling what his body senses and feels... You are just along for the ride... As if you can now understand his internal dialogue... what he says to himself while he is displaying this behavior or attitude... Take all the time you need and when you have made it through his day once again, let me know with a "yes" response. It's not necessary for you to see it, hear or feel it, just relax and imagine that it is all happening around you... you are doing perfectly. [Wait for the response.]

Wonderful... [Apply a tactile anchor during the next statement.] Now bring that experience into your own body and imagine using the resources you just experienced in your own past... That's right, go back in time and reorganize your thoughts and feelings of the past looking through the eyes of change... hearing through the ears of discovery... and benefiting from the realization that what the mind can conceive and believe the body will naturally and normally achieve...

Your thoughts become new things... your new concepts help to change and shape your perception of reality. Take the time to change your past... [Brief pause.]

What changes were made? How are these positive changes benefiting you in the future when you need them the most? Take all the time you need... When you have completed making changes to the past, give a "yes" response... [Wait for the response.]

Now that the changes are established in your past, think of things that will occur in your day-to-day activity that will trigger this resourceful new attitude. Think of the times and the places where you will benefit upon awakening... when you will be able to demonstrate a positive change... where a behavior of the past will be altered in such a positive and profound way that from this day forth you will constantly, on a day-to-day basis, make upgrades in your life experience.

Some of the changes will happen in the morning upon awakening... helping you feel fresh and alive... ready to lead a successful day of discovering who you are by developing who you desire to become... Some of the changes will happen in and through your day as you look back over successful encounters where you simply made the right decisions at just the right time...

You will find that as you enter into the deep stages of sleep, your other-than-conscious and powerful mind will make a review of your day and in that review will make all changes and modifications that would need to be made so that in the days, weeks and months to come you will be in a constant positive progression of change... All the things that you do well will now be even better... with the power of your mind. What your mind can do for you is no small thing, but it is a big thing that can be done in a very easy way...

So take a deep breath, relax and allow the positive processes of your mind to focus in on your future where you need the help the most... so that when you arrive, the changes will already be made... Take all the time you need to see, hear and experience the future and when you are convinced that the changes are made, and that your other-than-conscious mind will provide you with all the necessary behaviors and the correct attitude to reach your goal, just give me a "yes" response... and then go ten times deeper into relaxation...

Do you have all the resources you need to accomplish your goals? [If "yes" continue. If "no" you will need to guide the client through the Resource Generator technique here.]

You can use this technique both consciously and unconsciously. Your mind, that powerful resource which has always been there keeping you from harm, will remember this process so that in the days, weeks and months to come, if you come in contact with someone who displays a behavior or attitude that you would like to develop, even without your knowledge, you will simply begin to integrate the behaviors and attitudes that will help you become ultra successful in all areas of your life…

Take all the time you need to return back into the room… You can return only as slowly as your conscious and unconscious mind can continue to communicate and develop a greater perspective so that every day in every way life can get better for you… and this is so…

OUTLINE FOR USING THE UNLIMITED REALITY TECHNIQUE

1. *Start the progressive relaxation. Set up "yes" and "no" responses.*

2. *Have the subject think of someone who has the desired resource. Elicit a "yes" response when this access is made.*

3. *Ask, "Is this person a man?" If yes, proceed with references to "him" or "his." If no, proceed with references to "she" or "her."*

4. *Make the suggestion that the subject is following behind this person watching him move through a day of his life. From a distance the subject is watching and noticing everything about this person. Have the subject give a "yes" response when the day is completed.*

5. *Now have the subject imagine the day again, this time from within the person's body.*

6. *Bring the new discovery back into the subject's reality so that he or she can benefit from the information on a personal level.*

7. *Guide the subject into the future of his or her own life to discover where and when the resource could best be used.*

8. *Continue steps 1 through 4 until the subject has built the unlimited reality needed to attain his or her outcomes.*

9. *Suggest that the subject return back into the room only when he or she has reached full agreement to use this unlimited reality as a resource upon awakening.*

"If human beings are perceived
as potentials rather than problems,
as possessing strengths
instead of weaknesses,
as unlimited
rather than dull and unresponsive,
then they thrive and grow
to their capabilities."

BOB CONKLIN

Chapter Twelve

Quantum Fusion
Technique

The Quantum Fusion Technique is for the person who says, "I really want to change, but there is a *part* of me that just won't allow it to happen." When performing the Quantum Fusion technique we acknowledge this *part* that seems to be holding on to past behaviors and attitudes. Once acknowledged, it can then be *fused* with the part that strongly wants the change to occur. In reality, both parts are positive, or at least have underlying positive intentions. When the two are brought together, they are much more powerful than either one standing alone.

Most addictions or problem states have a counterpart. For instance, a middle-aged woman who has a 25-year smoking habit may say, "I really want to stop smoking, but there is this part of me that really enjoys the taste of cigarettes." I will first explain that she may honestly believe she enjoys smoking, but it is more likely that she trained herself to enjoy the taste, and it started from a positive intention – not positive to her body, but positive to her mind. For most people, the first inhale from a cigarette was a vile experience. Neophyte smokers usually feel sick, dizzy and often cough or gag. Somewhere along the line, however, they all "hypnotized" themselves to believe that it is an enjoyable experience. Thus, my favorite statement, *the law of mind is the law of belief,* rings true.

The problem is not that these people don't have the ability to stop smoking on their own. To the contrary, they have trained themselves to smoke, and enjoy it so much, they now need my assistance to stop. What they need more than anything is to stop focusing on the problem and begin to dwell on solutions. Sound simple? It is. While hypnosis is known for helping people change quickly, I think the combined science of Neuro-Linguistic Programming and hypnosis makes it possible to guide anyone to a successful change almost instantly.

I have discovered that the Quantum Fusion technique is extremely powerful for almost every situation. I use it with virtually all of my clients at one point or another. Incredibly, it can be used either in hypnosis or just as effectively outside a trance state.

I was once interviewing a potential hypnotist named "Judy" over lunch. She was an honest and enthusiastic young woman of about 30. I asked her if she had used any form of mind technology for her own personal growth. As a hypnotist, it's helpful to share personal stories with clients. It expresses one's own conviction in the power of hypnosis. Judy said she had used hypnosis to lose weight and was now eating healthy foods and living a healthful lifestyle. She then, rather sheepishly, admitted that she just couldn't seem to stop drinking coffee. Judy felt that her coffee habit didn't fit with her new health-oriented lifestyle, but she couldn't seem to give it up.

Since we were near the end of our meal, I asked Judy if she wanted a cup of coffee. She acknowledged that the end of a meal was her favorite coffee time. I summoned the waitress and soon Judy had a hot, steaming mug of fresh coffee before her and I had a cup of hot water for myself. As I took out my teabag (herbal from a health food store), I began to ask her certain outcome questions. I started by asking her just what life would be like if she were totally and completely coffee-free; what it would do for her. To my amazement, she began to describe, in detail, what her life would be once she was totally and completely caffeine-free. As she moved further along the storyline, getting lost in her new life, I recognized the signs that she was slipping into a light trance.

When she completed her story, I asked her, "What stops you from attaining this goal today?" She immediately began to tell me about "this part of me" that just couldn't seem to get anything done without the motivation and stimulation that caffeine brings. I stopped her here with a pattern-interrupt, by asking her to focus once again on her coffee.

I then placed my hands in front of me with the palms up. I explained that it was truly quite simple. "In one hand," I said, "there is a part of Judy who enjoys the taste, flavor and sensation of the coffee and caffeine. She acknowledged that this was correct. I turned one of my hands over and placed it on the table, then shifting my focus to the other hand. "And," I further explained, "there is another part of Judy who wants to be totally and completely caffeine-free." Judy was now nodding her head in agreement. "What are the positive benefits for Judy in being caffeine-free?"

She began to list them, one after the other. As she did, I made the impression that my hand was getting heavier, demonstrating that each time she listed a positive outcome it began to build a resource in my hand. She was soon watching the hand as she placed layer upon layer of resources in it.

I asked whether she could, just for a moment, step into that experience and live totally and completely caffeine-free. The moment she was there I turned my hand over. I glanced at the artwork above our booth and made mention of its beauty, breaking her state. I could then turn back to the hand holding the negative resource (the belief in the coffee), and said, "What does that part of you in the past really want?"

Instantly, without any hesitation, she said, "To get on with my life, to be motivated, and to do those things in life that I truly want to accomplish."

I asked, "Is there anything stopping you from doing that, as early as today?"

She let out a laugh and said, "Well, I'm drinking coffee right now!"

It was now my turn to laugh as I pointed out, "Maybe you didn't notice, but you haven't even sipped your coffee since it was served."

As I picked up both hands, palms up, and slowly brought them together I began negotiating between the two, I said, "There is a part of you who wants this change to occur, and that part of you is functioning in the future, now. And, there is a part of you who perhaps wants this change to occur, but it is functioning in the past, then."

As I continued to bring them together I brought her to the conclusion that it is perfectly okay for the past convictions, beliefs or concepts to be slowly integrated in the future – the future now –

which she will be living when she leaves this encounter.

"In truth, Judy, you don't have to make this change today. It can happen slowly," I said. "Some people simply discontinue drinking coffee on a certain morning upon awakening when they just feel good. There are mornings when you feel better than others, and it could, perhaps, be the day that would start a whole new life for you – the life you desire."

I then gave her the opportunity to expand her success by adding, "By becoming completely and totally caffeine-free, it will prove to your mind that anything is possible – as long as you believe it's possible.

I watched as she began to access the change and simply moved to other topics. As we broke up the interview, I noticed that her coffee sat untouched and had turned cold. As we parted, I asked her to give me a call sometime the next day.

When she phoned the following afternoon, she asked about the interview and the position at our center. I told her that I wanted her to come into the office for some hands-on interviewing in which she would perform hypnosis with a client. As our telephone discussion progressed, I sensed there was something more she wanted to say, but she hesitated and I didn't push it.

Upon arriving at the office, she almost immediately blurted out that she hadn't had any coffee since our meeting at the restaurant. I smiled and told her I thought that was wonderful. I then asked her whether she thought she could make it through the rest of the day without coffee. She shrugged her shoulders and stated that she really didn't think it would be a problem.

I promptly took her into the future with that attitude by asking whether she thought she could go through not only today, but maybe a week. "Would one week be enough time for you to be totally caffeine-free?"

She looked at me, a little puzzled for a moment, and then stated, "If I could make it three days it would be enough to convince me!"

"I'll look forward to hearing from you in three days then," I said.

Exactly three days later, I walked into the office early and the phone was ringing. Before I could finish speaking, Judy's excited voice came through the line announcing that she hadn't had any coffee for three days. In fact, she now is carrying herbal tea with her everywhere she goes so that she is prepared for any situation. I explained that it is the process of the other-than-conscious mind to plan, prepare and generate results. She acknowledged that this was just what had occurred for her.

I knew Judy now had the conviction that would allow her to become a good hypnotist and she did prove me right. After that, each time Judy and I went out to a restaurant together, we would both pull out our herbal tea bags and share a little laugh.

The main goal with most change technology is to get the subject to become congruent or unified in consciousness. As long as there is separation, there will be unconscious stress. It is the purpose of this technique to bring a person together through a *fusion*, so that all parts of consciousness are striving for the best possible outcome for the whole.

STEPS TO CREATING QUANTUM FUSION

Script For Quantum Fusion:

Go ahead now and close your eyes… take in a deep breath… let it out with a sigh… Take in another deep breath… This time as you exhale put your hands in your lap with the palms up. Be sure that the hands are not touching each other… Concentrate your attention on my voice… Allow all other sounds and all other voices to drift into the background of this session today… Each time you close your eyes with the idea of going into hypnosis, you will go deeper… it will be easier and more enjoyable each time…

Think of something that you would like to change about yourself… When you have done this, let me know by squeezing down with one of your hands… [Wait until you see the hand squeeze.]

Today that hand is going to represent the part of you that is responsible for that behavior… the behavior that you no longer want or desire… It is important that you realize that this part of you is not wrong... it is not broken... You created this part of you in the past for an important purpose... Today you will discover, at the other-than-conscious level, new ways to accomplish that goal... new ways that are just as immediate and more appropriate for where you are in your life today...

With this thought, go ahead and imagine the correct attitude... the appropriate beliefs... and all concepts that hold the old patterns... Now imagine the attitude, belief and concepts transformed into energy... Imagine the energy starting at the core of your brain... Imagine it flowing down across the shoulder and into that hand... the hand that represents the part that controls the patterns of the past... As this energy flows down the arm and into the palm of that hand, imagine it as a color... When you have built it into a ball of mental energy, just nod your head so that I know... [Once you see the head nod, continue. It is optional to reach over and anchor the inside of the palm with a tactile anchor. Then continue with the next statement. Let the anchor go at the end of the next paragraph.]

That's right, this is the part of you that controls the patterns of the past... It is not wrong or broken. Each time I mention the 'you of the past,' you will think of this hand and this part of yourself... Relax and go even deeper...[Let go of the anchor.]

From here move your attention down to the bottom of your feet... Notice how energy follows thought... Just as you thought of the feet and then the ankles, the blood flows freely there... Relaxation following thought... Let yourself go... Feel the flow of relaxation up through the legs as the hips relax... Now the lower part of the body is going loose, limp and completely relaxed...

Take in a deep cleansing breath... Imagine deep inside there is a part of you that is capable of solving the problems of the past... This part of you we will consider the 'you of the future'... This part of you knows your underlying positive intent and knows how to accomplish your goals in a safe, loving and wonderful way...

All you need to do is relax... Relax and imagine the correct attitude, beliefs and concepts for success... Convert them into energy... mental *energy… Imagine this mental energy moving from the core of the brain down across the scalp and facial muscles… flowing all the way down to the other hand… The hand that represents the 'you of the future'… the part of you that knows exactly what you need to see… what you need to hear… what you need to experience… As the mental energy flows down to the hand, it builds into a ball of mental energy… [If you anchored the other hand, anchor this hand as well.]*

When your hand has filled with a ball of mental energy representing this part of you in the future, give it shape, form and color…When you have done this, nod your head so that I know… [This is where you release the anchors.]

Notice the level of relaxation in the shoulders… Just moments ago I asked you to close your eyes… Imagine in one hand, the patterns of the past… In the other hand, the patterns of the future… In a moment these two different parts are going to agree to work together… from a deep, meaningful place at the other-than-conscious level. NOW… [This is where you will anchor both hands at the same time. This creates the fusion effect. Pause for 10 seconds until the integration is complete.]

From here these once separate parts will learn to work together… Even as you listen to my voice consciously, there is a part of you that is listening at the other-than-conscious level… That's the part of you that knows exactly what to do to bring these two together… It could happen physically… You could feel a magnetic effect as the two different balls of energy merge together… [This is where you release the anchors.]

Imagine the 'you of the future' journeying back through time… back to the beginning of time for you… back to the time when you would have needed these resources the most… Imagine how things could have been different… Imagine the 'you of the past' journeying ahead in time. Notice the day-to-day changes as you use more and more of your mind's potential…

As you listen to my voice, I want you to notice your body relaxing… each time going deeper than the time before… From this deep inner place, imagine the hands continuing to come together… This could be physical. They could come together and touch… Or it could be mental…

*The two balls of mental energy come together to form a new color...
Imagine this new color as if you are breathing it into your lungs...
then from your lungs to your bloodstream. Imagine in your mind's
eye that your heart is circulating these new ideas, these new concepts,
to every cell... every organ... every system of your body... As these
two different parts of you come together, you become more and more
aware of the 'new you'...*

*This 'new you' has all the skills of the past, has rehearsed the new
future, and upon awakening is willing to take the steps to be successful... This part of you understands the truth... The truth is that no
part of you is wrong or broken... The 'parts' simply need to be
retrained... trained to operate in a new time... with new skills...
skills that will help you accomplish your goals.*

*Each time you practice Quantum Fusion, you will find it more natural
to work within yourself... It is this incredibly flexible part of you that
I am speaking to today...*

*So this day you have decided to make a change... a positive change...
I want you to take these once separate, now together, parts of you into
the future... Imagine how they will work together... If there is a
problem in the past, you will dream of the solution in the future or
present... letting yourself go... If there is a problem in the future, you
will inventory your past skills and create a solution...*

*You are becoming solution-oriented... Everyday in every way you are
getting better... better... better and better than the day before...*

*Through the amazing power of your imagination, the past and future
have come together to help you attain your goals...*

*Fill your body with that new color. Imagine your body like an empty
glass container... Your body fills with this new color... your personal
color of power... so that when you see this color in your world it will
remind you of the decisions that were made here today... the decision
to live life in a state of harmony, peace and abundance... knowing
that all behaviors are positively motivated... and as your mind thinks
of the positive results of this process, other things begin to change...*

some of them are conscious to you and you recognize that a change has occurred… Most will be unconscious… you will simply be making positive and beneficial changes with no conscious effort at all. The motivation and desire will be generated unconsciously…

You can begin to slowly return into the room… but only as slowly as you can imagine the days, the weeks and the months to come… and when you come to that day in the future when you are convinced that all the changes are made, and that everyday in every way your life is improving, then you can open your eyes and return fully back into the room… saying to yourself 'wide awake, wide awake'… take all the time you need… And this is so.

OUTLINE FOR QUANTUM FUSION

1. *Have the subject relax and place his or her hands in the lap with the palms up.*

2. *Have the subject separate the polarities. The one hand represents the 'part of the past' and the other hand represents the 'part of the future.'*

3. *Have the subject give each polarity a color that best represents it. Reach over and anchor each polarity, breaking the state between each.*

4. **Now comes the fusion process.**

5. *Reach over and fire both anchors at the same time.*

6. **Let go of the anchors.** *Suggesting: Begin to think of the possibilities… if these two parts could somehow come together and help you accomplish this goal…*

7. *When the* **hands touch together suggest:** *Through the power of your mind, the past and future have come together to help you attain your goals…*

"Results!
Why, man, I have gotten a lot of results.
I know several thousand things
that won't work."

THOMAS EDISON

Chapter Thirteen

Mind Link
Technique

Although Quantum Fusion is one technique that you will probably use more frequently than any other, at times it is not appropriate to fuse resources together but rather to link them to each other. Advertisers do this all the time and quite effectively.

How do you spell relief?

If you said **R-O-L-A-I-D-S**, then your mind linked the Rolaids commercial with relief. The advertiser's intention was to take a negative state, such as intestinal upset, and link it with their product... *relief*. That's correct, their product is not really an antacid; their product is *relief*. *Relief* is what they are selling.

The Mind Link technique places the individual into control of his or her "state." In my experience, all successful people have one strategy in common – they know how to manage their mental state. Avoiding frustration is not the key. Rather, it is turning frustration into flexibility, fear into power, anxiety into expectancy, and so forth.

The Mind Link is effective for depression. People in a state of depression seem to fit a universal mold. Their shoulders are rolled forward and the head is down. This is where they are accessing feelings. People in a state of depression are typically going deep inside for an answer, where they know a solution is at hand. Depressed people literally withdraw from the outer world in order to put pressure on their deep inner resources. For this reason, I think a better term for depression might be *compression*.

By anchoring these people from the depressed state into one of possibility, their mind will instantly move from the state of depression to one of expectancy or perhaps even excitement.

I sometimes smile as I recall my first meeting with two psychologists who had asked me to write a program for the Driving Under the Influence (DUI) offenders in their state. They liked what I had to say, but they wanted me to prove that my techniques would work in the real world. They had shared a knowing glance, grinned and nodded, then gazed back at me. They knew who the perfect candidate would be. Her name was "Marcia," a young woman of 19 years who lived in a perpetual state of depression. They said that if I was able to help Marcia, I certainly had something that could help the world. I was up for the challenge, so I asked them to bring Marcia in.

Before I move on with Marcia's story I would like to make clear that those people in severe states of depression should always be advised to see a medical doctor. I was informed that Marcia had been thoroughly examined and had no physical causes for her depression.

The first thing I noticed was that Marcia's neurology was certainly that of the typically depressed. I asked her what was happening with her life. Her statements immediately told me that she had developed a dim and distant view of her future. There was nothing bright and compelling in her future that might have otherwise motivated her.

It would be impractical to attempt building a future from a depressed state. I knew the only way Marcia would experience results was if she could be moved from the depressed state into a positive one, where she could remain active and functional in life. The more she could move into the positive and uplifting state, the more she would accomplish, and the further she could move from the negative states of the past.

I began to train Marcia's mind to move from one state to another. I asked her to get into the depressed state. As soon as she had the feelings, I asked her to look up to the ceiling and think of three things she thoroughly enjoys doing. I told her to think of activities that have nothing to do with her present situation.

As Marcia looked up to the ceiling, a smile crossed her face, and she began to feel better, without knowing why. Her physiology began a transformation. Her shoulders rolled back, her head was up – she was beginning to look further down the road of life.

As soon as I recognized those signs of feeling good, I had her step into each of those situations and mentally live them to the best of her ability. Then, as I broke the state, I noticed that she was sinking back into depression, just as she had trained her body to do. I immediately took her back up to the ceiling with three new situations – this time in the future. Her eyes rolled up and instantly the lips curved into a smile and a look of health and vitality began to appear. Marcia's healthy, positive thoughts were triggering her brain to release endorphins that were making her feel good naturally. Once she went through all three future situations, I broke the state again.

As she looked around the room, I had her settle back in, and then turned to the two women to make a few comments. In these few moments, I watched Marcia slowly slide back into her depressed state, but this time, it was to a much lesser degree. Once again, I had her roll her eyes up, this time throwing her shoulders back. Marcia began to enjoy the game – the game of building excitement.

Marcia now realized that going after what she wants in life could be exciting. Internally planning and promoting success could feel like magic. It could become a form of addiction – a positive addiction – that improves the quality of everyday life. And the best part was, it could all be programmed, just like programming a computer, so that it happens automatically upon awakening in the morning.

I then told Marcia, "Your mind works perfectly. Instantly and automatically your mind can remember just what it's like when you roll your eyes up to the ceiling. I'm not sure how often you will need to do this process, but you are."

She promptly told me that, if she did it three more times, she would be pretty well convinced that it would work forever. I told her to go ahead and take herself through the same process three times, and when she was finished to let us know.

As we were deep into conversation about our future plans, Marcia's voice suddenly broke in. "I'm done," she chirped. We all smiled at her and continued about our business. Marcia sat and listened attentively. Her body remained erect and her eyes bright. Marcia had changed her thinking process simply by changing her body's posture. She had been able to link her mind to new experiences.

When I saw Marcia again only a week later, she was quick to point out how exciting and positive her life had become since she had learned how to use her to mind to instantly imagine what she wanted. She was now able to realize how, in the past, she had actually placed herself into the depressed state. She described how, after the first few days of practice, she began to change her states automatically, without even knowing what was happening. I told her that her other-than-conscious mind could continue this process and it would soon slide into an unconscious behavior completely outside of her conscious awareness.

Marcia had previously shown little motivation toward a career. She had bounced from job to job, each new position lasting only a week or two before she would quit or get herself fired. However, Marcia had built her own future where she is now successfully running her own business as a manicurist. She is frequently heard expounding on the merits of excitement and challenge in her work. She thoroughly enjoys being her own boss and making her own choices.

There are many situations where the Mind Link can come into play. Depression, stress, frustration or anger are the emotions that best respond to this technique. These are the states when a person feels out of control, with no excitement or movement toward goals. There is nothing worse than being stuck in a state and not knowing how to get out of it.

STEPS TO USING THE MIND LINK TECHNIQUE

Follow the simple outline below and transform failure states into powerful new triggers that boost creativity and productivity.

1. **Relax the client and set up "yes" and "no" responses using the index fingers.**

   Take a moment and close your eyes… start the relaxation response… breathe in deeply… breathe out completely… As you listen to my voice you will find yourself going deeper and deeper… Listen to each word that is said… Focus on my voice… Let go of all other sounds and influences... As you relax, you will use the right index finger for "yes" by moving it slightly and the left index finger for "no"... Each time you close your eyes, it will be easier for you to enter into the relaxed comfortable state of hypnosis...

2. **Have the subject think of an unwanted state. (Examples: anger, fear, frustration, anxiety.) Suggest:**

As you go deep inside, I want you to think of a state in which you feel 'stuck' such as fear, frustration or anxiety, Think of the state you would most like to change, and when you have that, give me a "yes" response.

3. **Get a full sensory anchor. Take the subject back to the earliest memory of this feeling. (Touch the back of the hand.) Suggest while anchoring:**

Now that you have a state that you would like to transform, begin to realize that you trained yourself to have this response... You now have the ability to learn a new response. Go inside and let your mind drift and wander back in time to the earliest memory that you can recall today of experiencing the unwanted state... It could be a memory as a child or it could be a memory of something that occurred as early as today. Move to that early memory and when you are there, let me know let me know with a "yes" response...

4. **Break the state.**
    Take a moment to notice that, each time I touch you in this way, you will remember this time and all of these feelings. And now you can open your eyes and look around the room... Take a deep breath and look around the room... That's right...

5. **Ask the subject to think of the opposite of the unwanted state or feeling.**

Take a moment now and think of what the opposite feeling or state would be... Think of a time in your life when you were in that opposite state... Fully get into this state... What were you seeing? What were you hearing? What feelings did you experience? Imagine that you are there now. What would it be like...? Give me a "yes" response when you have done this...

6. Get a full sensory anchor in a different place. (Touch the shoulder or opposite hand.) Suggest while anchoring in a different place:

   And now begin to realize that, each and every time I touch you in this place, you will immediately begin to think of the positive and beneficial resource... Remember the way colors look in your mind when everything seems to work perfectly... Remember what you say to yourself... Recall those wonderful positive feelings... let them fill your body... It's perfectly okay to feel good and accomplish your goals... When your body is full of these feelings, you can open your eyes and look around the room... (Let go of the anchor when the eyes open.)

7. Access the unwanted state (hold for at least 5 to 10 seconds), then trigger the opposite anchor and make the suggestion:

   What would it be like if the next time you began to feel this (the unwanted state) you immediately felt this (the opposite state)?

   Roll your eyes up as if you are looking up at three doorways... Each doorway has an opposite feeling and behavior from those of the past... these are positive new behaviors from which you can benefit as early as today... When you have this in your imagination, give me a "yes" response...

8. Once you receive a "yes" response, suggest while touching the positive anchor:

   Imagine that you are going through doorway number one... and instantly and automatically you begin to display a new behavior different from the behaviors of the past... Allow yourself to view this without question... stepping into the experience, seeing through the eyes of change, hearing through the ears of change and sensing and feeling with your body as if you were actually in the future displaying this new behavior... And when you are done, give me a "yes" response... (Release the anchor.)

9. Once you receive a "yes" response continue. Suggest:

   Step back out of doorway number one and step into doorway number two... (Press down again on the positive anchor)... Again, begin to fully experience this new behavior... Notice how well this behavior works in the future... Take all the time you need and when you are done, give me a "yes" response and step back out of doorway number two... (Release the anchor.)

10. **After the "yes" response, guide the subject through option number three. Suggest while touching the positive anchor:**

You have already been through two options that you could use to discover your outcome... so now step into door number three... Make this a behavior that you would perhaps never imagine yourself doing... Make this behavior even a little ridiculous and fun... This third door will be the door of flexibility... If there is a behavior between door one and three that might be appropriate in a situation, the other-than-conscious mind will provide it upon awakening... so move through this last doorway... See through your eyes of the future, hear through your ears, and sense and feel what your body would be feeling if you were to experience this state upon awakening in the future. Take all the time you need and when you have done this, let me know with a "yes" response... (Let go of the anchor.)

11. **Putting it all together.**

Now that you have seen, heard and experienced three new behaviors, begin to think once again of the unwanted state of the past... (Touch the anchor for the unwanted state while suggesting)... This is the past that you want to transform into a positive and resourceful state... When you have that state, give me a "yes" response...

12. **After getting a "yes," proceed by letting go of the unwanted anchor and touching the desired anchor and suggesting:**

Once again, what would it be like if the old feelings instantly and automatically brought about these new options...? Where you would instantly walk into each doorway and then decide which one would be best for you at that time...? Begin to think of three different situations in the future where this would be beneficial... (Pause.)

Now, in your mind, move in and through each door, discovering which behavior would be best for you. When you find that behavior, say to yourself. 'Yes, I will do that.'

Now think of three places in the future where you would want to display this behavior unconsciously... where the unwanted state could instantly be transformed into a positive new resource state. Take all the time you need and when that has occurred, imagine you are back in the room and give me a "yes" response (Release the anchor.)

13. **Testing the process.**

Suggest: When you think of the undesired state, notice what is it like now. Each time you practice this process, you will notice your eyes roll up... Instantly noticing the doorways of choice...

Test again after hypnosis. Watch the eyes when you ask a question about the stuck state. If the eyes roll from a feeling up to visual construct, there is a strong possibility that the new patterns are successfully installed. If not, continue to take the subject through step ten until you notice a definite state change, eye roll or both.

Remember that the purpose of this technique is to guide your subjects from a stuck or undesired state to a positive or suitable state where they will be able to make a different and more appropriate choice in behaviors or attitudes.

OUTLINE FOR MIND LINK TECHNIQUE

1. *Relax the client and set up "yes" and "no" responses using the index fingers.*

2. *Have the subject think of an unwanted state that he or she wants to change. (Examples: anger, fear, frustration, anxiety.)*

3. *Take the subject back to the earliest memory of this feeling. (Set a full sensory anchor.)*

4. *Break the state.*

5. *Ask the subject to think of the opposite of the unwanted state or feeling.*

6. *Set a full sensory anchor in a different place. (Touch the shoulder or opposite hand.)*

7. *Access the unwanted state (hold for at least 5 to 10 seconds), then trigger the opposite anchor. Have the subject roll his or her eyes up and imagine three doorways.*

8. *Trigger the positive anchor and suggest that the subject step through doorway number one. Release the anchor once the subject has imagined the experience.*

9. *Trigger the positive anchor and suggest that the subject step through doorway number two. Release the anchor once the subject has imagined the experience.*

10. *Trigger the positive anchor and suggest that the subject step through doorway number three. Suggest that doorway three represents something a little ridiculous and fun. Release the anchor once the subject has imagined the experience.*

11. *Ask the subject to access the unwanted state, while holding that anchor.*

12. *Let go of the unwanted anchor and touch the desired anchor. Suggest that the subject move through each doorway.*

13. *Test the process.*

"I am a kind of paranoiac in reverse.
I suspect people of plotting
to make me happy."

J. D. SALINGER

Chapter Fourteen

The Theater of the Mind *Technique*

In the 1970's, a technique called the Seven Minute Phobia Cure greatly influenced the widening popularity of a grassroots movement known as Neuro-Linguistic Programming. Since then, the technique evolved, was modified and spawned a variety of copycat methods.

Perhaps the founders of NLP could consistently accomplish results in seven minutes. In my experience, however, it depended upon the individual subject.

I believe the Seven Minute Phobia Cure is the best technique for demonstrating NLP's genuine ability to instantly and permanently modify behaviors. I have used this process with several hundred clients and have found that, in every case, the subject experienced a beneficial change. Unlike most NLP practitioners, however, I also guided the client through a hypnotic process to reinforce the new skills and abilities. Some NLP followers may argue that this isn't necessary. However, since I am in a referral business, I like to make sure the change is permanent. Also unlike other professionals in this field, the Positive Changes centers guarantee success.

At Positive Changes, we call our modified version of the Seven Minute Phobia Cure the Theater of the Mind. Why limit such a powerful technique to phobias? I have seen it work effectively for anger, panic attacks, anxiety, weight loss and more. The Theatre of the Mind is for any client who feels stuck or says, "I'm out of options."

When I first started in the field of hypnosis, I had a group get together at my house every Tuesday night to discuss the latest mind techniques and processes. On one particular evening, after guiding the group through what I perceived as a pleasant hypnotic experience, I noticed that one person, "Thelma," looked upset and puzzled. When I finally asked her what had happened to upset her, she started crying with deep, racking sobs. I could tell that Thelma's weeping was unnerving to the group, but I allowed Thelma to cry as I went around the class and discussed each of their experiences. I then asked the class to go on break. They all took the cue and went to another room.

I was now able to ask Thelma about what had happened to so thoroughly upset her. Thelma told me that she had a snake phobia and that during the hypnotic session, for some reason unknown to her, she had imagined being attacked by snakes. She could think of nothing that would have prompted this mental image, but it was clear that it had upset her greatly.

Fortunately, I was in the midst of my NLP training and had just learned to work with phobias. I knew the Theatre of the Mind technique could work for Thelma, but I would have to be flexible since she was in such an agitated state.

I stepped Thelma through the process and found that, as she released the *synesthesia* (reaction) of the mind to the image and internal stimuli, she was creating a distorted mental impression far worse than reality could ever be. In her imagination, innumerable snakes were slithering over her and biting her, yet she had never even seen one.

In NLP, the term synesthesia literally means, "a synthesizing of the senses." At this point, Thelma was unable to separate the thought of snakes from her sensory reaction to them. In other words, Thelma was seeing, hearing, feeling, tasting and smelling the experience as if it were really happening and with maximum intensity.

After I took her through the Theater of the Mind, Thelma was able to return to the class with a smile. Her eyes reflected inner serenity. She was feeling wonderful and positive – much to the disbelief of the others in the room. They couldn't believe this was the same woman who, just minutes earlier, had been wracked with sobs. She now appeared rested, relaxed and confident. Although the group was clearly puzzled, no one spoke up at the time.

At the next week's meeting, Thelma explained to the group that, when she had gone home a week ago, it was the first time she was able to walk through her home without the fear that snakes were slithering across her floor, a nightmare with which she had lived since childhood. She said that she felt more free, confident and peaceful than ever before.

Another example of how the Theater of the Mind can work came when I was doing a hypnosis demonstration for a friend at a local event she had sponsored. There were a variety of demonstrations and lectures going at the time. Some local television and radio personalities got together and decided they were going to do a show proving that hypnosis wasn't real. I was scheduled to do one of my stage hypnosis demonstrations in which I put a few subjects into the hypnotic state and have some fun.

As I walked through the crowd after my show, a woman named "Jane" stopped me. She had read my biography and had noticed that I was an NLP practitioner. Her purpose in intercepting me was to bluntly inform me, "That NLP stuff doesn't work."

I responded with, "What do you mean it doesn't work? Everyone works perfectly!" I further explained that NLP is the "science of people" and its intent is to help people improve themselves and their lives.

I then asked her how she had come to such an uncompromising conclusion about NLP. She explained that she had gone to an NLP professional (one for whom I had great respect), who had taken her through the phobia technique. "It failed completely," she sighed.

I asked her to stay at the event until I completed some business so I could discuss her experience further. I told her that I would like the opportunity to show her just how well NLP would work right there in the night club. Jane's husband had been listening in on the conversation and as I turned to walk away he handed me a small, plastic spider. "Try throwing it on her sweater," he said. "I guarantee you'll see a phobia!"

I knew that, for the Theatre of the Mind to bring about a phobia release, there would have to be a true phobic reaction. The technique works for basic, fear-based problems as well, but is performed in a slightly different way.

Later, when I returned to Jane, I said "Hello," and reached out to shake her hand. I flipped the spider onto her sweater. Sure enough, she had an intense phobic reaction. I don't think Jane appreciated my little test much, especially when her husband was standing a few feet away roaring with laughter.

I guided Jane through the Theatre of the Mind technique. Because her reaction had been so strong, however, I didn't let it end there. After she had been through it once, I asked her whether this was the same method as the other NLP practitioner had used. Her reply was a sly, "Yes."

I now knew I would have to do something *more* and *different* to convince her conscious mind that it would work this time.

I told her we were now going to do something a little more diverse. Since she had done it once, and then done it again, she could now split the screens in her mind so she was seeing the situation in two separate places. As I took her through the process, I noticed her eyes accessing the memories on the split screens. Slowly she showed signs of relief. The phobic situation was beginning to have less and less impact. With these signs of success in my hip pocket, I continued the process until she had so many screens of time, encountering so many different spiders, that in her other-than-conscious mind, she had probably met every spider that could possibly enter her life experience from that moment on.

When I finished the process, she seemed somewhat confused, so I went about my business and made a point to see her later, with my friend the plastic spider.

When I threw the spider at her this time, she caught it, looked at it and said, "I knew it was plastic."

I reminded her that she knew it was plastic before, but it hadn't stopped her from reacting. I reinforced the new behavior by telling her that I would give her a call a week later to find out how well it was working, "When I call, you can tell me about all the marvelous positive changes you are experiencing in your life just because you overcame this one phobia," I said.

Since that encounter, Jane and I have become friends. To this day, Jane will tell people how she got rid of her phobia in a noisy nightclub filled with hundreds of people and the media.

To be truly proficient with this or any of the Psycho-Linguistic patterns, you must be flexible within the structure of the techniques. Most of your subjects will have little or no knowledge about hypnosis, NLP or the techniques you are using. You are the expert! Just as I changed the technique to fit Jane's needs, you, too, can make alterations to fit the needs of the clientele you see.

Your first step will be to uncover whether your subject is accessing a true phobia or is simply living out a fear-based reality. It is imperative that you notice the reaction to the negative anchor. Some hypnotists even keep rubber snakes, spiders and other paraphernalia of common phobic reactions. What is most important is that you, as a hypnotist, have a concrete concept of what that phobic reaction is for your client.

One way to inspire a phobic reaction is by the simple mention of the word. In a true phobia, the person will begin to tremble, the face will flush, or you may be presented with a look of absolute horror. The best test is to simply bring up a situation wherein the reaction has occurred in the past. Then watch closely. When looking at a true phobia, there is a noticeable physiological change.

STEPS TO USING THE THEATER OF THE MIND

Before hypnosis:

1. **Access the phobic state. (Test to verify the fact that what you are dealing with is truly a phobia. Time has proven that this technique works best for phobias, however, it will also work on fear, anxiety or any other unconsciously motivated behavior.**

   When was the last time you experienced the phobic reaction? (Get a full sensory anchor.) Go inside and then describe to me what you were seeing and hearing... What did your body feel like? (At the peak of the experience, set a tactile anchor.)

2. **Have the subject disassociate and think of all the possible positive reasons for having this phobia. Discuss how this phobia perhaps is protecting him or her in some way. Review the ecological reasons for the phobic reaction.**

Return your awareness to the room... Now let's think of this phobia in a new and different way... Let's assume that this behavior is motivated by a positive intention... that something positive is trying to be expressed deep within you...

Because you had this phobic reaction in the past, in what positive way could it be working for you? Is it perhaps keeping you from harm or helping you to learn? Use your creative mind to think of all the possibilities... possibilities that are positive. It does not matter whether the underlying reason is true or not... just allow your creative mind to think of a list of positive reasons for the past behavior... Know that whatever the real positive intention is, it will always be met... only now and in the future it will find a positive and beneficial outlet... one that will allow you freedom from the past phobic reaction... Take all the time you need to discover the positive underlying intention... And when you have it, let me know so we can continue this session...

3. **Set up "Yes" and "No" responses and elicit responses after each step.**

   Close your eyes and become aware of my voice... allow my voice to become smooth and comfortable for you.... It is from here that with each and every word that I utter and each and every breath that you take, you will go into a peaceful positive place for change... So with that, I want you to use this finger for a "yes" (reach over and lift one of the index fingers).... relax and go deeper and deeper to that perfect state of relaxation for you... Now I want you to use this finger for a "no" (lift the index finger on the other hand... And go deeper and deeper with each and every response...

4. **With eyes closed, have the subject imagine himself or herself in a theater, comfortable and relaxed.**

   Now that you are becoming more and more comfortable, I want you to imagine the inside of a theater. It could be a theater that you have visited, or one that you are just now making up for the purpose of this session... It really doesn't matter... When you have created this theater in your mind, give me a "yes" response so that I know and we can continue this process...

5. Have the subject imagine a black and white snapshot of himself or herself on the movie screen before the phobic reaction starts. (It could be a time in the past or a time in the future.)

Imagine now that the curtain is being drawn back and on the scene is a black and white picture of you... this is a black and white picture of you before the phobic reaction starts. You are sitting back in one of the seats in the theater watching the scene over there... And on that scene there is a black and white picture of you before the phobic reaction starts... it could be a past or future time. When you have this image in your mind, give me a "yes" response.

6. Now have the subject imagine that while sitting and watching the picture on the screen, in a still picture, that he or she floats out of the body in the chair and into the projection booth.

As you imagine yourself watching the black and white image of you on the screen... you begin to float out of your body sitting in the chair and you float up to the projection booth where you can now imagine watching yourself down in the chair, watching yourself on the screen, in a still frame snapshot in black and white. You will stay in the projection booth until you are given the suggestion to leave...

It is from here, as you look down out of the projection booth, that you can see yourself watching yourself on the screen and begin to think of all the skills and abilities you will need in the future to overcome this old behavior. When you have made a mental list of all the behaviors and the correct attitude you will need, give me a "yes" response and go deeper and deeper...

7. Have the subject imagine that the black and white image is coming to life so the new behaviors and attitudes will be sequentially programmed for success.

You are now watching yourself watch yourself and you will stay in the projection booth as the black and white snapshot begins to turn into a movie... This is not just any movie; this is a movie about you moving through the phobic reactions of the past... The movie can begin now in black and white... As you watch yourself down in the seat in the movie theater, watching yourself on the screen going through the experience of the past... And when you have made it successfully through the experience, give me a "yes" response so that I know...

8. When the subject gives you the "yes" response, have him or her jump from the projection booth into the scene and have it fill with color.

As you have now made it through the experience, imagine yourself jumping from the projection booth into the image on the screen... Now take a deep breath of relief and begin to color the picture... place sounds around you and experience those wonderful feelings of knowing that you have made it... Fill yourself with the emotion of that experience... Like an empty glass container, fill your body up with these positive emotions... And when you have done this, and have the feelings of making it, give me a "yes" response...

9. Get a full sensory anchor and have the subject imagine that all the images, sounds and feelings are going quickly in reverse while bringing up the feelings of knowing that he or she is going to make it. When the subject is back at the time before the phobic reaction starts, have the subject give you a "yes" response. Suggest as you reach over and set the anchor:

Now imagine that you are going back through time. Imagine that all the scenes and all the sounds are running in reverse... That's right... everything you remember occurring during and after the phobic reaction of the past... I want you to imagine that everything is going in reverse... and when you are back at the time before the reaction of the past was triggered, open your eyes and return back into the room (release the anchor)...

10. When the subject returns into the room, test the process by suggesting:

Now when you think about the phobic reaction of the past, what occurs?

Note: Calibrate the difference in the response.

11. **Find out how many times the subject feels that he or she would need to go through this process so that it will work unconsciously as early as today.**

Because you have been through the process once, you can remember the steps and now see yourself in the scene, in black and white, before the reaction of the past… Watch yourself float up out of your body and into the projection booth. When you are in the projection booth, start the film. When you get to the point in the scene where you know that you have done it… when you know that you have taken all the steps to protect yourself and have kept yourself from harm, just jump into the scene… Feel the emotions of knowing that you have made it… fill yourself up like a glass container… then move back through time in reverse as fast as you can, faster than before… And when you have done that again NOW… open your eyes and return fully back into the room… here and now, where the positive underlying intention has been modified… in such a powerful and positive new way that this new behavior will be where you need it the most, just as you need it… and this is so… [Pause]. Take all the time you need… But before you open your eyes, think of three places in the future where you could benefit from using this technique…

12. **Ask the subject to go through the process five times on his or her own and let you know when it is completed.**

Because we have done this once… and you have reviewed this process once again… you have really done this process twice, and again just NOW… So now go back through the process five times and watch yourself with the new resources… opening your eyes and looking around the room between each process. Remember to run the process in full color in reverse as fast as you can… When you have done the process five times, let me know with a "yes" response.

13. **Once this process is completed, break the state again. Ask:**

Are you sure you have done the process five times?

Note: *The subject should go up and review the process five times to make sure that it has, in fact, been accomplished.*

14. Ask the subject what it is now like when he or she imagines the phobic reaction of the past. If you witness any phobic reaction, have the subject do the process three more times. If it appears that the reaction has been appropriately changed, you are done. Continue to step 15.

15. Have the subject practice and future pace.

When is the next time you will be in a situation where you can test this process?

Allow the subject to give you a response, then suggest:

What is the future going to be like now that you have this new resource at work for you? Close your eyes and imagine the days, weeks and months to come and just how nice it is going to be now that you have this new skill and ability.

I say to you now... every night as you drift off into a dreamy, drowsy state of sleep, your other-than-conscious mind is going to take this information into your dreams... As you begin a sequence of dreams that will bring about the success of your life and this program, you will sleep deeply and rhythmically, knowing that your mind, and what it can do for you, is no small thing, but it is a big thing, that can work for you in a very easy and simple way...

I say to you now... you will begin to dream of all the possibilities... of everything that could or would occur in your future... and this time, begin to think of just how this new process is going to fit in unconsciously so that you will be unaware that it is even occurring... in the same way you are unaware of the part of you that is presently beating your heart or controlling your breathing... this new process has already gone back through time... through the memories of your past... changes have already been made... powerful and positive changes that will simply work for you in the days, weeks and months to come... changes that will convince you that everyday and in every way life is getting better for you... and this is so.

Take all the time you need to integrate this new behavior so that instantly and automatically, through the rest of your life, it will be there keeping you from harm... Take all the time you need to move to the day when you're convinced that all of this is working for you... When this has occurred, open your eyes and return to the room... take all the time you need... the seconds are like hours... the hours become days... and the days flow into weeks... take all the time you need NOW to return back into the room...

"I've got to keep breathing.
It'll be my worst business mistake if I don't."

SIR NATHAN MEYER ROTHSCHILD

Chapter Fifteen

Swish Pattern

"Steve's" foot tapped furiously as he at once tried to explain his nail biting habit and hide his gnawed fingertips. When Steve finally held out his hands, I was amazed to find that he had bitten his nails to the quick and there were tiny droplets of fresh blood oozing from his cuticles.

"Doc," he said, "Do you have any experience in helping people stop biting their nails? I'm so embarrassed by my hands, but I can't seem to stop."

I told him to rest assured that I knew of a process that would likely work in seven minutes or so, at least that's what the developers of the technique claim. "And I'm living proof," I said, while offering Steve a view of my own neatly trimmed fingernails. "While I was learning this technique, I used it myself to kick my nail biting habit," I said. "I haven't chewed on them since, and that was about ten years ago." I admitted to him that my nails were nowhere near the shape his were in, but that the habit had embarrassed me as well. I, too, felt that my chewed nails were unprofessional.

"That's just it, Doc," he exclaimed. "I work in the medical field and, although I'm pretty successful, this rotten habit is holding me back."

After enrolling Steve, I informed him that he would likely require just one session to overcome his nail-biting compulsion. I explained that the remaining sessions in his program would be to assure his life-long success and could also be used to build his self-confidence or achieve other goals. "I don't believe in one-session programs," I told Steve. "Biting your nails is a symptom of a greater problem within your subconscious mind. Together we will solve that problem. Over the next few days, I would like for you to think of anything else you would like to work on in your personal life."

I explained to Steve that hypnosis would offer him the tools and techniques to solve these problems on his own. I then asked, "Would you be willing to take the energy you once put into biting your nails and convert it into building new resources specifically for accomplishing your goals?"

"Absolutely," Steve readily agreed.

"So Steve," I said. "Help me to understand your nail-biting habit. Do you find yourself biting your nails at specific places or specific times?"

"It's whenever I don't have something to do with my hands." He thought for a moment and added, "It seems my hands find their way to my mouth automatically. Pretty soon I'm chewing away without even knowing it."

"What other methods have you used to try to stop?"

Steve thought for a moment. "Well," he said. "When I was a kid, my mom tried putting some nasty tasting stuff on my nails. You won't believe it, but I actually started to enjoy the taste of it." He paused. "I also tried to will myself to stop, but that lead to nothing but frustration. In fact," he said, "I think it made it even worse. I'd be really embarrassed if my friends noticed just how bad it's become lately."

"What is the positive benefit of being free from this problem?"

Steve's eyes lit up. "I would be able to proudly show off my work."

Steve explained that his job is in the dental industry. He creates beautiful crowns that finish off root canals or dental implants. His crown and bridge company was one of the leading providers in the area. He had very little contact with the public, but frequently entertained dentists and oral surgeons. He admitted that he had begun dreading the meetings, his embarrassment over his hands was so great. I asked, "What do you think their response will be when your nails grow out?"

"Well," he said, "No one has ever said anything about it, but I know they notice. Most of them have well-groomed nails. Not too many professionals bite their nails. I think that when they notice I've stopped, they'll have more respect for me."

I immediately jotted down the word "respect," since this was clearly an impact word for Steve. "Are you ready to get started," I asked. With Steve's firm "yes," I proceeded to ask an important ecology question. I wanted to know if he knew the secondary gain to biting his nails. "Is there any reason you shouldn't stop biting your nails?" I asked.

Steve couldn't think of any reason. If he had, I would have worked it into the session. "If between sessions you think of any reason, please let me know," I said. "I must warn you, at first this may seem a little like the Three Stooges."

"What?" He asked with his eyes wide.

I put my hand directly in front of him and said, "It's going to seem as if I am about to push a pie into your face. But don't be alarmed. The point of the exercise is to break the pattern. In fact, in the hypnosis world, they call the process just that, a pattern interrupt.

Step Number One

I had Steve picture an image of himself on the tip of my finger. I asked him to imagine himself there with his shoulders rolled back and his chin upward. He is smiling and presenting one of his beautiful pieces of dental work for inspection. "It is actually too small for you to see at this moment," I said. It is just a speck on my fingertip. Are you willing to imagine this?" I asked him. He agreed.

I suggested that as I moved it closer to him with a swish, the image became bigger and brighter. I stopped my hand about 6 inches in front of his face. I then asked him to describe a situation, in detail, when his shoulders were rolled back, his chin was rolled upward, and he was smiling. I then asked him to look down at his fingertips and describe for me what he was seeing. Steve described his nails as naturally manicured and well groomed. At that point, I dropped my hand and created a break state by asking him to look around the room.

All learning happens through spaced repetition and sequencing. Within all the patterns of Psycho-Linguistics, there is a sequence. Through the repetition of the sequence, there is spaced repetition. This allows the memory of the new experience to move from the conscious mind to the other-than-conscious mind as quickly as possible, registering the result as useful information to be applied by the client upon awakening.

There is also a theory called Chunking. This theory states that a person can only handle so many chunks of information at any one time. Theorists say the average individual can manage a range between seven and nine chunks of information at one time. So think of each of these chunks as a piece of the puzzle. As clients learn each piece, they put it together into an unconscious and automatic mechanism. The first chunk of this process was to teach Steve about his true self, put it at the tip of your finger, and rapidly move it toward him with a swish.

Step Number Two

I set up the process the same as in Step Number One, with my hand stretched out in front of him. I then suggested that on the tip of my finger was the image of Steve, totally successful in overcoming his compulsion to bite his nails. I then asked Steve to remember a time when he was biting his nails. The moment he felt the desire to lift his hand, I urged him to go ahead and allow his hand to lift. The moment his hand began to lift, I moved my hand, still with the image of the successful Steve on the tip of my finger, quickly toward him, saying the word swish, and then stopping my hand again 6 inches in front of his face. I then suggested that he put his hand back down in his lap, close his eyes, and imagine three places where he would want to remember to promptly forget about biting his nails.

Step Number Three

I then asked Steve, "How many times do you think you would need to do that before you could permanently interrupt the pattern of the past?"

Steve thought for a moment and then responded, "At least six times."

I then suggested that he put his hand out in front of him (the same hand he had lifted when he had the urge to bite). I touched his index finger and suggested that he imagine an image on the tip of that finger of himself, proud of how his nails have grown out and thrilled with the well-groomed appearance of his hands. I then asked him to once again get into that state where he found his hand wanting to lift up toward his mouth. I told him, "As soon as you notice the hand moving, quickly take the hand extended out in front of you and move it toward your face, saying the word out loud, swish, just the way I did it before." To make Steve comfortable with the process, I actually did it along with him. Together, we repeated the process six times. Between each event I made sure that Steve did a break state, by asking him to shake his body and then looked around the room.

Step Number Four

It was now time to test the process. I turned, looked directly at Steve and asked, "It's the future and your hand is moving up toward you, what happens?" Immediately I notice his head tilt back slightly as he states, "I will put my hand back down by my side."

While Steve's verbal answer was helpful, the tilting back of his head when he accessed the information was the cue I was looking for. I now knew that his other-than-conscious mind was accessing the Swish Pattern.

"Would you be willing to practice this Swish Pattern every morning until the desire to even think about biting your nails is gone?"

When he agreed, I knew he was now ready for the hypnosis process. As a hypnotist, you will think of practicing the Swish Pattern outside of hypnosis as preparing your clients for what they will experience during hypnosis.

"Steve," I said. "During your hypnotic process, I will be using the term swish. At that moment you are to imagine everything we just did. Agreed?"

"Agreed," stated Steve.

THE SWISH HYPNOSIS PROCESS:

Script for the Swish Pattern:

Go ahead and take a deep breath in. With your eyes comfortably closed, follow along with my voice. Let each breath go with a sigh... just let go of everyday thoughts and experiences. Notice that, through this natural breathing process, the sensations in your scalp, facial muscles and tendons go loose, comfortably limp, completely relaxed... so relaxed and comfortable that any outside sounds... any outside experiences… only cause you to refocus on my voice… allowing my voice to resonate between the right and the left side of the brain. My voice is now becoming smooth and comfortable for you.

Notice how this transition into relaxation deepens as you shift your attention to your shoulders. Lift the weight of the world and place it behind you. Just let go. There is no place you need to be… nothing that needs to be done at this moment in time. The only thing you need to remember is to relax along with my voice and let yourself go. Notice how the arms, all the way down to the fingertips, relax. You might be feeling a lightness… you might be feeling a heaviness… it might be a tingling sensation. No two people experience hypnosis in the same way. All you really need to do is relax. Let go and let it happen.

Shift your attention to your breathing… breathing in deep relax-ation… breathing out all stress… all tension. Notice your heartbeat… rhythmic, natural and automatic. I mention your breathing and your heartbeat, because they are both controlled by the other-than-conscious part of your mind. It's the part of your mind with which you are learning to integrate the Swish Pattern. It's the part of your mind that will notice, with your awareness or without your aware-ness, your hand moving up toward your face, and at the right moment… at just the right time… swish… the new you will then enter your mind. This is the part of you that knows… knows how proud you will be of your nails as they grow out naturally… and you take care of them. So this will be so, notice the rising and falling of your chest… as the chest, abdomen and back go loose, comfortably limp, completely relaxed… so relaxed and comfortable that whatever you need to see, hear, and experience to integrate the Swish Pattern becomes natural and automatic in your mind… programmed into your thoughts, and effortlessly a part of your nature upon awakening. So this will be so…

Notice the hips and thighs going loose, comfortably limp and com-pletely relaxed. Even as I am speaking, your other than-conscious-mind is planning just where and when you will need the Swish Pattern the most. Knowing that the more you practice, the better it will become, and the better it becomes, the more natural it will be. Each

*time you practice this Swish Pattern, you will find the old sensa-
tions… the old pattern… melting away…eliminating itself from your
experience. Each time it is easier than the time before.*

*Become aware of your total body relaxing from the knees and calves
to the ankles… even the balls of your feet… every cell, system and
organ of your body… relaxing comfortably. From this inner space of
peace and comfort, I want you to imagine the next 24 hours of your
life. As you imagine the next 24 hours, notice your hands comfortably
by your side. Become aware of each time your hands move up toward
your mouth… then instantly, automatically, without question…* **swish**
enters into your mind.

With this thought of **swish** *in your mind, immediately your shoulders
roll back, your chin moves upward, and you begin to breathe the way
you will breathe when you know success is guaranteed. You then remember to forget… by forgetting to remember… all about biting your
nails… so that the old thought will no longer be necessary… it will
no longer be a part of your thinking process. This could all happen
today… it could happen tomorrow… it might have already happened.
All you really need to do is relax and benefit from the power of your
own mind.*

*With this thought, imagine the next 24 hours… and think of three
different places in the next 24 hours where you want the Swish Pattern
to work freely for you. (Pause and allow the subject time to think of
three different places.)*

*From here, recognize the level of relaxation you were willing to attain
today… knowing that each time you practice relaxation, you will go
just a little bit deeper. It's time to take a mental vacation… and on this
mental vacation, you will dream of all the successful ways that you will
use the Swish Pattern upon awakening. When you next hear my voice,
it will not startle you all. In fact, it will only cause you to go deeper…
deeper… deeper… inside your own mind. (Pause for 20 seconds.)*

*As you become aware of your body's level of relaxation… knowing that
you're learning self hypnosis in a powerful, positive way to improve
your life… all you will need to do to reach this level of relaxation is*

close your eyes, take a few deep breaths, and remember the sensation you have right now. With that feeling, you remember how to go this deep... or deeper... on your own. If you're listening at a time of sleep, continue your journey into the deepest realm of sleep, where you incorporate the Swish Pattern into your dreams. You might find it convenient, just before awakening... swish... your mind remembers that, upon awakening, your true self awakens within you.

You might find that, when you reach over to turn on a light switch... swish... instantly your true self enters into the room with you. Some people find it convenient, the moment they turn on the shower to wash their body, just before the water hits against their skin... swish... they're cleansing their minds of all negative thoughts, all negative concepts, all negative beliefs. They are ready, willing and able to accomplish their goals of the day.

One may find that the days transform into weeks... and the weeks into months... I say to you now, if you are listening at a time or place where you need to be awake, alert and conscious, I'm going to ask you to slowly return into the room... but only as slowly as you can find the value in using the Swish Pattern... Once a day is good... twice a day is better... and three times a day is excellent.

When you're ready to comfortably and confidently allow your nails to grow out... without question or hesitation... your eyes will open and you will become wide awake... feeling fine and in perfect health... feeling better than ever before... and this is so.

OUTLINE FOR THE SWISH PATTERN

Set up the Hypnosis Process

1. Have subject think of the compulsive behavior he or she wishes to change.

2. Have subject imagine himself (herself) on the tip of your finger. Suggest that this image is of him or her smiling, with shoulders rolled back and chin up.

3. Move the image closer to the subject with a **swish**, and suggest that it is getting bigger and brighter. Hold finger about 6 inches from subject's face.

4. Have subject describe the future when the unwanted behavior is gone.

5. Break the state.

6. Have subject imagine himself (herself) on the tip of your finger, this time totally successful in overcoming his or her compulsion.

7. Have subject recall a time when he or she displayed the compulsive behavior.

8. Move hand forward with a **swish**, suggesting that the subject close his or her eyes and imagines three places where he or she would want to remember to forget the compulsive behavior.

9. Ask the subject how many times he or she would need to display freedom from the compulsion for it to be permanent.

10. Have the subject perform the Swish Pattern using his or her own finger.

11. Do the Swish Pattern with the subject based on the answer is Step 9.

12. Test the process.

Reinforce the Swish Pattern with Hypnosis

1. Relax the subject.

2. Give suggestions that the subject will automatically use the Swish Pattern at just the right moment.

3. Have subject imagine the next 24 hours and how many times he or she experiences the Swish Pattern happening automatically.

4. Relax the subject further, then suggest that he or she think of three different places where the Swish Pattern will be used in the future.

5. Future pace.

"Thoughts lead on to purposes;
purposes go forth in action;
actions form habits;
habits decide character;
and character fixes our destiny."

TYRON EDWARDS

Chapter Sixteen

Producing Analgesia Through Glove Anesthesia

The science of hypnosis gained ground in the medical arena in the mid-1800's when a few daring surgeons tested and proved its effectiveness in painless surgery.

In the early part of the 19th Century, surgical skills advanced rapidly. Most people, however, risked surgery only when certain that death was the only alternative. Why? Imagine yourself going under the knife while wide-awake and fully sensitive to pain. In my case, I'm sure it would take several attendants just to hold down my arms and legs!

Dr. James Esdaile, a Scottish surgeon practicing in India, decided to try mesmerism (the commonly known name for hypnosis at the time) as a means of pain control during surgery. He was not completely successful at first, but later perfected his technique and performed numerous operations without any disturbance on the part of his patient. Esdaile performed amputations, removed cataracts, tumors and enlarged toenails, and performed at least seven surgeries for fluid buildup in various body cavities. At a time when the surgical mortality rate was 40%, Esdaile reported a rate of just 5%. He attributed his success to mesmerism, which successfully relieved his patients of pain.

Dr. Esdaile had discovered *analgesia,* the body's natural ability to produce anesthesia. Esdaile was delighted with his breakthrough. He had hoped that one day the benefits of mesmerism would be widely known.

Just six months after the publication of Esdaile's book, *Mesmerism in India, and its Practical Application in Surgery and Medicine* (Esdaile, 1846/1977), William T.G. Morton applied an ether-soaked sponge to a dental patient and removed a dental tumor without the patient showing any signs of pain. Within two years, ether, chloroform and other chemical anesthetics were widely used in dentistry and medicine. Esdaile's brand of mesmerism was lost to history.

There are many purposes for modern hypnotists to produce hypnotic anesthesia for their clients. One such use is to help a subject who has a fear of the dentist, which is, in reality, a fear of the potential pain. A subject who is allergic to chemical anesthesia may find hypnosis a welcome alternative. Pain-free childbirth is another use; and the list goes on.

In relation to the results achieved, the technique seems almost unbelievably simple.

OUTLINE FOR GLOVE ANESTHESIA

1. Ask the subject to close his or her eyes and imagine the eyes cannot open at all.

Notice that your eye muscles and tendons are going loose, limp and totally relaxed. In fact, so loose, so limp and so totally relaxed that you won't be able to open them at all. In your mind's eye, imagine rubber bands lying on a tabletop... they are loose and limp. Then imagine your eyelids are equally loose and limp... you eyelids are to- tally relaxed. Concentrate your attention on your eye muscles and tendons... and notice that they won't open at all... and when they are that relaxed, just try to open them. Notice the harder you try, the more difficult it becomes... It's just too much work and you stop trying...

After the subject has tried to open them, move to number 2.

2. Suggest:

> *Now that you are relaxed, I'm going to have you count in reverse from 100 to 0 and each and every number is going to take you deeper than the number before... When you reach the number 97, all other numbers will drop from your mind, drop from your thoughts and drop from your awareness.*

3. Start the counting process:

> *Client: 100*
> *You: Deeper and deeper, the numbers are dropping.*
> *Client: 99*
> *You: Deeper and deeper, the numbers are dropping.*
> *Client: 98*
> *You: Deeper now... as the numbers are dropping.*
> *Client: 97*
> *You: Let the numbers go now...*
> > *out of your mind and out of your thoughts.*

4. After client has lost the numbers, suggest:

> *I'm going to move your hand and when I do I will drop it back into your lap. Let it fall loose, limp and completely relaxed... like a wet dishrag... loose, limp and relaxed... completely and totally relaxing.*

> *Continue to drop the hand into the lap until the hand and arm drop loose and limp like a dishrag.*

5. Choose one of the subject's hands and state that you are going to apply a little pressure. As you apply the pressure with a very slight pinch, ask the person if the pressure is being felt. When the subject acknowledges the pressure, let up on the pressure. Move on to "a."

    a. *Stroke the back of the other hand suggesting:*

> *Numb and anaesthetized... going completely and totally numb and anaesthetized. (Continue stroking the hand and repeating this suggestion.)*

b. *After a few moments, tell the subject that you are once again going to apply a little pressure. Pinch the hand that you anesthetized hard enough to leave marks. Apply a small amount of pressure to the other hand. While doing each hand state:*

A little pressure, let me know when you feel a little pressure.

6. Count the subject out:

1... 2... 3..., eyes open... look around the room. Notice the marks on your hand.

After you have applied the pressure to both hands and pinched the one hand leaving a mark, count the subject up to awakened consciousness. Have your subject notice the marks on the hand that was pinched. Chances are your client will be extremely surprise since he or she probably felt only a light pressure. Your client is now easily convinced that the same analgesia that allowed only the feeling of pressure as you applied the marks, can also be used for whatever purpose your client has chosen; whether you are guiding him or her into a state for painless dentistry or a surgical situation without anesthesia.

Again, there is a multitude of deepening techniques, and this is only the pre-testing process for producing glove anesthesia. After you have done the test and have confirmed the subject's ability to create glove anesthesia, the appropriate hypnosis session is to be applied. In this way, the client can be guided into a state of total numbness and anesthetization throughout the entire body. Of course, in a situation where the process is being used for a medical or dental procedure, the process should be done under the physician's supervision.

"My creed is that:
Happiness is the only good.
The place to be happy is here.
The time to be happy is now.
The way to be happy is to make others so."

ROBERT INGERSOLL

Chapter Seventeen

Guide to Auditory and Visual *Entrainment*

It was a balmy winter day in Phoenix in 1987. My education was nearing completion and I was eager to start my own hypnosis practice. I had only one problem. I knew nothing about running a business. My college courses had not taught me how to get a new enterprise off the ground. I paced the floor, turned to my dad and sighed. "We need a partner," I said. "We need to hook up with someone who knows how to run a business."

My father and I were having one of our many discussions about hypnosis. That's when Dr. Paul Adams' name came up. While living in Michigan, Paul had been a mentor to my dad. We also knew that he had a thriving multi-location hypnosis practice in the Detroit area. Dad said that Paul was scheduled to visit his parents in Phoenix later that month. I urged my dad to call him to set up a meeting. During Paul's visit, we struck a deal to help him open an office in Phoenix.

On a scorching summer day shortly after the grand opening of Positive Changes in Phoenix, I attended a hypnosis convention in Las Vegas, Nevada. I was rushing to the next event when a woman's voice called out to me. I turned to glance at the woman who was standing in front of a booth, an odd electronic device was perched on the table behind her. I had intended to wave her off, but the strange gadget made me stop to take a look. The woman was Linnea Reed. Behind the booth sat her partner, Larry Gillen. The device was called the Sensory Input Learning System (SILS). One of my early loves was electronics, so my curiosity was piqued. "Would you like to go for a ride?" Linnea asked.

"Sure," I replied.

I was directed to sit back in a lawn chair. Linnea handed me a set of earphones and sunglasses equipped with small lights. "I'll let you go about ten minutes," she said. "Just close your eyes and have a great trip."

Not knowing what to expect, I settled into the chair and closed my eyes. Within moments my senses were assailed with flashing lights and rhythmic tones. I immediately felt a sense of relaxation and wellbeing wash over me. Yeah, I thought, I could get into this.

By the time the session ended, I was blown away. I had never before felt so relaxed. I didn't want to move. "Come on," came Linnea's voice. "The group is about to take a break. You need to get up."

"That was the most amazing ten minutes of my life." I said.

"Ten minutes? That was more like 45 minutes. You seemed to be having such a good time, I decided to let you keep going."

"Wow! It seemed to go that fast," I said, snapping my fingers. "I've got to have one of these machines. How do I go about buying one?"

"Well, you're in luck, I happen to sell these things... and they're only $10,000."

My heart sank. As a new business owner, it might as well have been $10 million. Yet I had never let money stand in my way before. I simply had to own one of these amazing devices. The wheels in my mind began to turn.

As fate would have it, Linnea and Larry relocated to Mesa, Arizona. I followed them around to their many events and soon a friendship was formed. We soon struck a bargain. I would sponsor them into my clinic on the west side of Phoenix where they could offer demonstrations of the machine and, between performances, they would leave the machine with me so I could research the benefits with my clients.

I had once again accomplished a goal, and it hadn't cost me a dime. I had set no limitations on possessing the machine and had, therefore, visualized and realized my goal.

Since I started using light and sound technology in 1987, every Positive Changes Hypnosis client has had the chance to experience this life changing technology.

Over the years light and sound technology improved dramatically. In 2003 we decided it was time that Positive Changes designed its own light and sound relaxation system to perfectly match the needs of our clientele. Although machines no longer cost $10,000, they can range in price from strobe light machines, which have no therapeutic value, for $170 or less to clinical models costing $5000 or more. We set out to create the best machine at the lowest possible price. Our goal was to integrate the best of what's out there and design a unit that would cost our clients around $200. After reviewing the research, testing nearly every device on the market, and finding the right manufacturer for our Positive Changes Light & Sound Relaxation System was born.

HOW IS LIGHT AND SOUND TECHNOLOGY APPLIED?

Light and sound technology, also known as *auditory and visual entrainment,* is introduced to the brain through the ears and optic nerve using computerized technology applied through headphones and specially designed glasses equipped with light-emitting diodes (LEDs). These lights flash at predetermined frequencies and are coupled with binaural tones through the headphones. The auditory and visual entrainment is typically synchronized, but can be varied depending on the desired effect.

The rate of flickering light affects the brain by way of the optic nerve and causes the brainwaves to *entrain* or match the set rate of flickering to a desired frequency. The method by which this entrainment occurs is known as *Frequency Following Response (FFR)*. Unlike biofeedback, where the user attempts to intentionally calm or train brainwave activity, light and sound induced *entrainment* occurs directly to the brain without the conscious effort of the person.

Within minutes of use, the mind begins to follow the same frequencies of the light pulses and sound beats. The FFR helps the mind develop focus, reduces inner chatter and helps the individual relax quickly and easily. Because this is a *learned response*, the effect is cumulative. After a few weeks of regular use, it trains and balances the mind and helps the user remain calm, focused and alert even when faced with high-pressure situations.

While light and sound technology can be beneficial to most people, it is not for everyone. Persons with epilepsy, any type of seizure disorder or any visual photosensitivity are advised against using a light and sound device. People who have a pacemaker, suffer from a heart disorder, have a history of serious head trauma, or are taking stimulants, tranquilizers, or psychotropic medications, including alcohol or drugs, should consult their physician before use. Anyone experiencing dizziness, migraine or severe anxiety after using light and sound should discontinue using the device and consult a physician.

WHAT ARE THE BENEFITS OF LIGHT AND SOUND TECHNOLOGY?

Whenever people ask me why we use light and sound technology in the Positive Changes centers, I tell them one of my favorite jokes. It goes something like this: One evening a man in a tuxedo rushed up to a street musician and asked, "How do you get to Carnegie Hall?" Without skipping a beat the musician answered, "Practice, man, practice!"

Hypnosis works because it involves *mental practice* or *spaced repetition*. In my opinion, there is no faster or easier method for achieving spaced repetition than through the synchronized rhythm of light and sound.

The induction into higher brainwave states increases brain activity, while the induction of lower brainwave states reduces hyperactivity and feelings of anxiety. Brainwave entrainment within alpha states, for example, allows relaxation and a decreased stress response to occur by providing a slower and more relaxed brainwave state.

A faster brainwave state produced by faster flickering of the LED lights, induces a higher brainwave state, and is theorized to provide enhanced brain stimulation and increase cognitive abilities. In many cases, a faster brainwave state can decrease hyperactivity, similar to the paradoxical application of neurostimulant medications such as Ritalin, and Dexedrine.

The following results have been demonstrated
through a variety of studies:

- *Increased Long and Short-Term Memory*
- *Increased Attention-Span and Concentration*
- *Reduction of Anxiety and Depression*
- *Reduction of Medication Intake*
- *Increase in Right-Left Visual-Spatial Integration*
- *Major Increases in Creativity and Ideas*
- *Aids Decision Making and Holistic Problem Solving*
- *Decreases Migraine or Headache Frequency and Intensity*
- *Reduces PMS Symptoms*
- *Reduces Insomnia and Sleep Disorders*
- *Improves Motivation*

Each time an individual experiences deep relaxation through
rhythmic lights and tones, the following benefits occur.

- *Blood flow to the brain increases, which results in clearer thinking, better concentration, improved memory and enhanced creativity.*

- *Serotonin levels increase by 21%, which calms the mind and body and creates an overall sense of well-being.*

- *Up to 100% of excess adrenaline is eliminated – excess adrenaline could otherwise be toxic to the body.*

- *Endorphin levels increase by 25% – these are the hormones that flow through the body when we feel happy.*

- *When combined with hypnosis, your mind is filled with positive images and affirmations. Your mind learns to conceive of, and believe, new thoughts that are easily achieved.*

- *20 minutes of light and sound relaxation can be equivalent to 3-4 hours of sleep. Consequently, you may find yourself sleeping less, feeling more rested, accomplishing more during your day, and basically enjoying life more fully.*

Most people would pay thousands of dollars for a magic pill that offers the kinds of benefits I've outlined here. You can give yourself or your clients these same results in just 20 easy, relaxing minutes.

I hope you will feel welcome to pick up the phone and call 1-877-POSITIVE. Your local Positive Changes Hypnosis Center will be happy to give you a free light and sound demonstration. Please tell them Patrick sent you.

"The only way to discover the limits of the possible is to go beyond them into the impossible."

ARTHUR C. CLARKE

Chapter Eighteen

Psycho-Linguistics and You

I believe Psycho-Linguistics is the new frontier of psychology. We are living in a fast-paced, high-tech society – one that wants rapid changes. Nightingale-Conant and other audio manufacturers have created a billion-dollar industry out of motivating people.

Now, too, self-motivation is becoming a major part of psychology. Those of us in the people-helping professions will quickly find the archaic method of hour-long personal encounters in the psychological setting left behind as the demand for rapid change increases. Quick, easy techniques that go directly to the core of a behavior are fast becoming the therapy of choice.

People are becoming more and more aware of the benefit in creative visualization, imagery, hypnosis, Neuro-Linguistic Programming, meditation, prayer and positive thinking. Additional rapid-change processes, like those found in this book, are developing every day and, as these methods prove effective, are gaining credibility. Thus, greater change will occur on the planet as a whole.

I am convinced that the work I am doing, along with thousands of other therapists and trainers, is a catalyst in an amazing shift for humankind. I am pleased that you've chosen to join us.

HOW DO YOU ALIGN WITH THE HYPNOTIC MIND?

The dialogue that follows is for you, the hypnotist. Woven within the words is the mind-set for excelling as a Psycho-Linguistics practitioner. Simply record the transcript into your computer or onto a CD, using the power of your own voice, give yourself a preparatory mind treatment before going into a session.

Quiet your mind and focus deep, deep inside. Focus on your breathing by noticing how one set of muscles is breathing in… and the lungs themselves respond by naturally releasing out. So it is with the mind… You are able to listen to your clients and allow the intuitive mind to invent the sessions that would be most appropriate for each individual client to experience. You are using all the skills of the hypnotic mind to monitor the breathing of the client. You will naturally notice how your breathing coincides with that of your client.

And… naturally… you will notice the eye accessing cues…. How when the eyes roll upward, the subject is accessing visual information… and when the eyes roll from side to side, the client is accessing auditory pieces of information… and when the eyes roll downward, you will know that kinesthetic information is being processed. And… naturally… you are always willing to calibrate and test these assumptions because you know that the process of hypnosis is one of pacing and leading… leading your clients in the direction of their goals.

During each session, you will discover how your mind can become clear and focused. Each session is a new session… and the hypnotic sessions of the past are now resources that will help you to build the constructive future that you desire.

Once again, take in a deep breath… and notice how this deep breath helps cleanse the body all the way down to the bottom of the feet… and the feet and ankles go loose, limp and completely relaxed. Now, feel the grounding of information from al books you have read, all seminars you have attended, all positive pieces of information that could possibly help you to use your intuitive, hypnotic connection to create a session that is most appropriate for the client at hand. Notice the power of relaxation flowing through you. Perhaps you are now beginning to recognize how everything that happens through you must also happen to you. Therefore, each suggestion is positively stated in the affirmative.

Now you may be noticing how the calves and shins are relaxing... so relaxed and comfortable that flexibility moves into the knees. You are flexible and open to the possibility that through you today, a process or technique that may have never before been spoken, could be, and perhaps will be, spoken through you. Open your mind to the possibility in guiding your clients through whatever "stuck state" they may find themselves in, and to the accomplishment of their goals.

Trust that you will recognize your clients' outcomes and selectively hear their impact words as you ask the questions: What would you like? Where would you like it? How often would you need to display the new behavior, and with whom? Both consciously and unconsciously, you will remember to check the ecology in each idea or concept... and your negotiation skills are naturally improving. You will be noticing both conscious and unconscious cues that will allow you the consistency you desire for your session. Each time you enter into a hypnosis session, to create the optimum communication possible, you will notice that your body will remain relaxed and comfortable. You will be guiding your client through the pacing and leading process into such a deeply relaxed, positive state that outside sounds and influences will only prompt you to remain more focused on the task at hand. You will allow the information to flow to and through you.

Now you may want to notice how the thighs and hips are relaxing. Concentrate, using your mind's eye, on how the client will walk in and how comfortable you will feel greeting him or her. Notice how you are able to use all the rapport skills you have built over time... and how your rapport skills are getting better and better. In meeting your client, you remain comfortable and relaxed and you feel confident in each word that you speak. Your rapport skills are so fine-tuned that your body matches and mirrors in exactly the right sequence, tone and tempo for you... you are doing perfectly. You are getting the taste of Psycho-Linguistics and noticing the smell of success. In your mind's eye, concentrate on how you will lead your clients from confusion into a state of focus and balance.

You will find yourself naturally future pacing each technique as the days become weeks... and the weeks become months... and the months become years. You will continually scan the situation to notice all visual cues... all auditory cues... and all kinesthetic cues that will help you provide the information necessary to complete the hypnotic sequence. Each time you enter a hypnosis session, your quality will improve... your ability to produce results will improve... and as you mentally imagine your subject in the relaxed and natural altered state, you will notice that as the subject's eyes close down, and with a few deep breaths, you will guide your client deeper into a positive and productive state known as hypnosis. Your skills with hypnotic language patterns will improve... you will notice the flow of each word and with every new session, the words will flow more consistently in the direction of a deeply relaxed and positive state.

In a moment, my voice is going to pause. During this quiet time, I ask that you imagine the complete session taking place. You may choose to use the Quantum Fusion technique, where the part of the past and the part of the future merge together to create the dynamic moment known as now. Perhaps you will choose to use the Mind Link technique to link resourceful, positive states in less-than-positive behavior patterns. Allow your mind to focus on the possibilities of double disassociating in the Theatre of the Mind technique as you watch yourself over there on a screen of space... watching yourself relaxed and comfortable and noticing that all skills, abilities and resources you need will flow to you and through you as you need them the most during the session. I don't know exactly which of the techniques you will need to use today... but you do...

As you move through the process... simply take a few deep breaths and scan your body... notice how you are keeping the positive thoughts resonating through your body as the hands and arms relax... the chest, abdomen, back, neck and head all relax. When you have completed the sequence of how your client will be guided through all the procedures that will bring about success... then notice how your *client leaves your office... Notice how positively your client has responded... and how positive you feel. You know that you did the very best you could, given the information you had available. From here you will take the time to review the session and create all other probabilities for success so that each session will improve upon those you performed in the past.*

I'm now going to pause so that you will have all the time you need to finish the sequence of thoughts that will structure a positive and resourceful session and bring about the results your client desires... Then, and only then, will your eyes open... at that point, you can return to the room and full conscious awareness.

HOW DO YOU RE-CHARGE THE HYPNOTIC MIND?

The next transcript is for use at the completion of your sessions so you are always upgrading the programs in your hypnotic mind. The process will clear your mind of any negative feedback that may have been part of the session. Record this guided imagery in our own voice. You may wish to record one tape with your pre-session process on one side and this post-session process on the other. Each will help you assess your hypnotic approach and keep your mental battery on full charge.

Take in a deep breath... and let that breath out with a sigh. Notice the calm between the right, creative side of your brain and the left, analytical side of your brain. Notice the way your mind and your body are creating a cleansing from within by using each new breath now.

Breathe in the color white... breathe it in and mentally wash from your mind all thoughts, ideas and concepts about the session. Become neutral with every piece of information that was shared... whether the information was positive or negative, just let it go. By mentally recharging the body, you can become neutral to the experience. As you breathe in deeply, once again, mentally recognize how you can make a deep, meaningful connection with the therapeutic mind. Whatever you will need to see, hear or experience to learn from the session you just administered, or from any prior encounter, will naturally flow into your awareness... and at just the right time.

Notice how the facial muscles and tendons respond to the positive suggestions to relax now. Feel how the relaxation moves into the face and flows back into the scalp. As the scalp relaxes, you may be noticing just how productive your body can feel in a deeply altered state of relaxation. This soothed and comfortable response can then move down through the neck and shoulders... lifting the weight of these past experiences from your shoulders. Whatever you said during that session... whatever you experienced and whatever you perceived as your client's experience... imagine the new possibilities now awakening in your mind as you use that positive information for yourself. Imagine what type of connection you might have had with that person... What possible purpose could you have had when drawing that individual into your experience? Was it to create a clearing for yourself? Perhaps to make your own positive changes right along with your client?

In your mind's eye, notice how everyone with whom you are associated is somehow connected with you through beliefs, habits or patterns. Notice how you are helping others to develop an awareness of their full potential. Activate your inner ability to imagine that you are relaxing comfortably in the same position in which your client rested and relaxed. Can you imagine the possibility of using each positive suggestion for yourself? Imagine the way the arms to the fingertips will respond upon awakening if each positive suggestion could be applied in your personal life. Whether or not you have the same "problem" as your client is irrelevant... is it not? Imagine that your mind could take you deep, deep inside to select a behavior, attitude or belief that could change or improve through the use of the suggestions given to you by your client's experience... because you have already discovered how all that happens through you must happen to you... have you not?

Notice how the mental energy flows down through the chest, abdomen and back... clearing your body of the experience... and allowing you the empowerment necessary for handling each new client with *resourceful skills that will only get better. As you allow the days to become weeks… and the weeks to become months… you can mentally imagine the many ways in which this session could have been different. After you have reviewed the session once in your mind, I want you to review it once again, but using different techniques and suggestions. Perhaps you will discover a body movement that was consistent, but of which you were previously unaware. Once again, you can notice the tone and tempo of the client's language patterns and how you can pace with a comfortable match. You may even be able to notice just how your client's hips, thighs, knees and shins relaxed and how your hips and legs are now releasing into a deeper level of relaxation.*

As you drift off into the world of deep, meaningful possibility, just take a deep breath in… then let that breath out with a sigh and allow yourself the experience of your favorite meditation or place for relaxation. Imagine the possibility of building a garden in your mind… a beautiful, peaceful place with the fresh scent and calming sounds of nature all around. Imagine the taste of deep, deep relaxation moving into your mind as you gain a flavor for the experience. You are naturally clearing the filters of your mind's eye to see the golden shaft of the sun beaming down and into the top of your head, burning away any negative thoughts, beliefs or influences. Allow the delicate, white clouds to float overhead… representing your true self image. Right here and right now you are establishing the truth for you, and for every one of your clients… that every day and in every way we learn and discover just what we need the most.

As the days in your mind become weeks… and the weeks transform into months… and the months flow into years, imagine the vastness of a blue sky in your perfect place of relaxation. Notice how the blue sky extends in all directions… adding to your mind an expanded view of the session you just completed. From that place, drift off into a dream where you can create the possibility of going back through time to the very beginning for you… taking the information you experienced today along with you. Can you feel how your past is being upgraded from what you have discovered today? And how you are now reinforcing your connection to the hypnotic mind?

I'm going to pause now. This quiet space is for you to allow your mind to move through time in the direction of your goals... at times you may be mentally reviewing the future... making all the changes and enhancements that are needed to mentally, physically and emotionally recharge you hypnotic mind...

You will have all the time you need to finish the sequence of thoughts that structure positive and resourceful sessions and bring about the results your future clients desire... Then, and only then, will your eyes open and, at that point, you can return to the room and full conscious awareness... refreshed, revitalized and anticipating your next opportunity to help another person as you help yourself.

"If you had faith
even as small as a tiny mustard seed
nothing would be impossible."

MATTHEW 17:20 LB

I hope you always remember that practice is the very best teacher of all. When performing Psycho-Linguistics, you cannot do harm as long as your intentions are for helping others and you are continually directing your clients toward their goals. Always move with ecology – staying in tune with the thoughts, feelings and ambitions of your clients. With this foundation, you will effectively lead your clients just where they want to go.

"The least of learning
is done in the classrooms."

THOMAS MERTON
US religious author, clergyman, & Trappist monk (1915-1968)

BIBLIOGRAPHY

1. Andreas, Steve and Connirae; *Change Your Mind – And Keep the Change*, 1987, Real People Press, Moab, Utah

2. Alcoholics Anonymous World Services, Inc., *Alcoholics Anonymous*, 3rd Edition, 1976

3. Bandler, Leslie Cameron, et al.; *Know How*, 1985, FuturePace, Inc., San Rafael, California

4. Bandler, Richard and Grinder, John; *Frogs Into Princes*, 1979, Real People Press, Moab, Utah

5. Braid, James, M.R.C.S.E., C.M.W.S&c, *Neurypnology*, 1843, John Churchill, Edinburgh, Scotland

6. Dilts, Robert; et al. *Neuro Linguistic Programming: Volume I. 1980*, Meta Publications, Cupertino, California

7. Erickson, Milton H., MD; *Life Reframing in Hypnosis*, 1985, Irvington Publishers, Inc., New York, New York

8. Erickson, Milton H., MD; *Time Distortion in Hypnosis*, 1982, Irvington Publishers, Inc., New York, New York

9. Erickson, Milton H., MD; *Experiencing Hypnosis*, 1981, Irvington Publishers, New York, New York

10. Gilligan, Stephen G., *Therapeutic Trances – The Cooperation Principle in Ericksonian Hypnotherapy*, 1987, Brunner/Mazel, Inc.

11. James, Tad and Woodsmall, Wyatt; *Time Line Therapy and the Basis of Personality*, 1988, Meta Publications, Cupertino, California

12. Kostere, Kim and Malatesta, Linda; *Get the Results You Want: Neuro-Linguistic Programming*, 1985, Metamorphous Press, Inc., Portland, Oregon

13. Metos, Thomas H., *The Human Mind – How We Think and Learn*, 1990, Franklin Watts

14. Porter, Patrick K.; Positive Changes, Inc., *Information Brochure* Copyright 1990

15. Rushkoff, Douglas and Wells, Patrick, *Free Rides – How to Get High Without Drugs*, 1991, Bantam Doubleday, Dell Publishing, New York, New York

16. Weitzenhoffer, Andre' M.; *General Techniques of Hypnotism*, 1957, Grune & Stratton, Inc.

"I am ready to meet my Maker:
Whether my Maker is prepared
for the ordeal of meeting me
is another matter."

WINSTON CHURCHILL

Your Franchise
Opportunity

Are you looking for a rewarding, people-helping profession that also fulfills your entrepreneurial and financial dreams? Positive Changes is waiting for you!

Positive Changes Hypnosis® Centers is a unique, all-inclusive and gratifying business opportunity that is taking the self-help industry by storm! We are actively seeking people who believe in the power and success of Positive Changes' programs to join our growing network of franchise locations. Together we can offer affordable assistance to people seeking to make lasting lifestyle improvements.

Positive Changes is meeting a demand as North America's first and only franchised network of hypnosis professionals. Our success is based on our one-of-a-kind programs, products and testimonials from those clients whom we have helped along the way. By offering more than 160 various pre-recorded hypnosis programs, we provide client services for virtually any problem.

We provide all of our franchise owners with thorough training in the operation of their center, hypnosis training and a complete franchise package that will support you in opening your center and running it day-to-day. To get started, all you need is the desire to succeed and we provide the rest!

Our amazing business formula is uniquely Positive Changes and is a result of years of research and operational testing. As an owner, you will be provided with a proven step-by-step program used in all Positive Changes centers across the U.S. and Canada. You will be supplied with everything you need to operate your center.

As you are well aware, consumers in the self-improvement industry are extremely focused on results. At Positive Changes, we have set our services apart from the rest of the self-improvement pack, offering consumers something new, long lasting and effective. Recognized by the American Medical Association, hypnosis is an effective method of behavior modification that is non-psychological, 100% safe and has no side effects. Over the years, we have gathered moving testimonials and photos from weight-loss, smoking and other clients who have had great success with our services. We will supply you with these testimonials, a suggested advertising schedule, marketing materials, a Positive Changes newsletter, state of the art website, direct mail campaigns and much, much more. Testimonials are the driving force behind getting new clients through your door. We'll even show you how to effectively gather testimonials from your own clients.

Because of the success and presence of Positive Changes and its franchisees, the market for consumer hypnosis services is expanding. A franchise provides you with many advantages like extensive training, access to recognized logos and brand names, strong marketing materials and advertising power.

The Positive Changes corporate experts will train you, provide you with assistance in finding the right location for your center, recruit and train your staff, provide tools, forms and checklists you need for daily operations and much more! We will show you how to form partnerships with local doctors to gain referrals and how to retain current clients, while growing your list of new clients. In other words, you will receive everything you need to run a successful center.

What are you waiting for?
Positive Changes is ready for you!

To receive a franchise information visit our website:
www.positivechanges.com

Positive Changes Franchise Headquarters
4390 Tuller Road
Dublin, OH, 43017
Phone: (614) 792-8100

1-877-POSITIVE / www.positivechanges.com

7 Keys to Weight Loss Mastery®

Learn to eat and think like a naturally thin person, conquer your cravings, increase your self-confidence, and plan for a lifetime of weight loss success! Here are just a few of the 52 titles available!

- *Develop the Characteristics of Naturally Thin People*
- *End Roller Coaster Weight Loss*
- *Evaporate Cravings and Hunger Pangs*
- *Extinguish Sugar and Chocolate Addiction*
- *Convert Your Body into a Fat-Burning Machine*
- *Changing Eating Habits and Food Preferences*
- *Exercise – Your Key to Lasting Energy*
- *Establish Lifelong Eating Habits and Patterns*
- *Change Diet Saboteurs into Diet Supporters*
- *How to Eat Out Every Day and Still Lose Weight*
- *How to Have Your Cake and Lose Weight, Too*
- *Go to HypnosisToGo.com for the complete list of 52 titles*

Hypno-Quit® Smoking Cancellation System

Kick your smoking habit for good using the proven strategies in this series. Conquer your cravings and extinguish the stress and frustration associated with quitting smoking. Break the chains that have bound you to cigarettes and be tobacco free forever!

- *Avoiding the Usual Quitting Traps*
- *Eliminate the Anchors That Create the Habit*
- *Relaxation and the Non-Smoker*
- *Tobacco-Free at Work*
- *Conquer Cravings and Be Tobacco-Free*
- *Extinguish Stress and Frustration*
- *Going with the Flow Tobacco-Free*
- *Tobacco-Free By the Numbers*
- *Planning a Lifetime Tobacco-Free*

Mind Mastery™ Series

Choose the hypnosis processes that best suit your needs for creating limitless personal change and success in your life. Ask about our discount when you purchase all seven!

- *Activate Your Personal Success*
- *Put a Dead Halt to Self-Sabotage*
- *Keys that Create Success*
- *Trying New Things*
- *Stimulate Optimistic Thinking*
- *Building Motivation and Drive*
- *Release Fear & Doubt*

Pain Free with Hypnosis

Overcome the hold pain has on your life with these hypnotic processes that teach you to manage pain using the most powerful pharmacy on Earth – your subconscious mind!

- *Freedom from Pain*
- *Awaken Pain-free*
- *Planning Your Future Pain-Free*
- *Freedom from Discomfort*
- *Tapping into the Most Powerful Pharmacy on Earth*

Hypno-Learning® Series

Overcome learning challenges with this amazing series! Increase your reading speed, improve your memory, get organized and earn better grades with our complete learning system.

- *Increase Reading Speed and Comprehension*
- *Activate Your Perfect Memory and Recall*
- *Getting Organized and Finishing Projects*
- *Enjoy Public Speaking*
- *Quick Tricks for Student Genius*
- *Goal Programming and the Successful Student*
- *Self-Confidence and the Student Genius*

Sales Mastery Series

Discover the powerful selling methods of sales masters! Build your self-confidence, master your time, and learn to overcome objections, with this amazing series.

- *Self-Confidence in Sales*
- *Beyond the Cold Call is the Sale*
- *Prospecting is Fun and Profitable*
- *Create Your Plan and Work Your Plan*
- *Think Big and Realize Your Sales Goals*
- *Sales Success Self-Hypnosis (So-Hum)*

Hypno-Golf® Series

Discover how hypnosis can enhance your enjoyment of the game you love! Use this tape series to mentally rehearse your success and instill the right mind-set before you play. Learn simple techniques for improving poise and concentration.

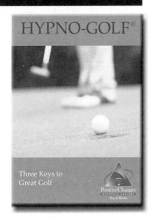

- *Course Management and State Management*
- *Three Keys to Great Golf*
- *Goal Setting for Golf*
- *The Golfers Mind*
- *Eliminate Hidden Strokes*
- *Mental Practice for Better Golf*

Psycho-Linguistics®

Enjoy the luxury of self-hypnosis any time you desire once you've mastered the art of self-hypnosis. This audio set makes learning to hypnotize yourself easy and fun! You can use the techniques to improve your life in 1,001 different ways!

- *Ten-to-One Method of Self-Hypnosis*
- *Three Easy Steps to Self-Hypnosis*
- *"So-Hum" Self-Hypnosis Process*
- *Psycho-Linguistics Class: Dissociation as a Resource*
- *Psycho-Linguistics Class: Resource Generator Technique*
- *Psycho-Linguistics Class: Compelling Future Technique*
- *Psycho-Linguistics Class: Resource Organizer Technique*
- *Psycho-Linguistics Class: Unlimited Reality Technique*
- *Psycho-Linguistics Class: Quantum Fusion Technique*
- *Psycho-Linguistics Class: Mind Link Technique*
- *Psycho-Linguistics Class: Theater of the Mind*
- *Psycho-Linguistics Class: Glove Anesthesia*

Hypno-Delivery® Series

Bringing a child into the world is probably the most amazing and life-altering of all human experiences. Sadly, for many women, the joy of the experience is lost due to fear, stress and pain. Now, with the discovery of the mind/body connection, women have an alternative – hypnosis. This series is designed to help the mother-to-be let go of stress, relax and enjoy the entire process of pregnancy, delivery, and motherhood. The listener is taught to use the power of thought before and during delivery to create an anaesthetized feeling that transforms pain into pressure.

Titles for Hypno-Delivery include:
- *Planning Your Pregnancy Stress-Free*
- *Mental Toughness/Emotional Readiness*
- *Healthy Lifestyle/Healthy Baby*
- *Mental Skills for Hypno-Delivery*
- *Balancing Your Life During Pregnancy*
- *From Frustration to Flexibility*
- *Visualize & Realize Your Hypno-Delivery Goals*
- *Preparing for Motherhood*
- *Self-Hypnosis for Successful Hypno-Delivery*

Call and your local Positive Changes Hypnosis® Center to ask about this exciting program, and how you can participate.

**1-877-POSITIVE or PositiveChanges.com
HypnosisToGo.com**

Mind-Over-Cancer® Series

If your thoughts could boost your immune system, would you be interested in learning how? Are you curious about the mind/body connection and its link to healing? Would you like to know how your mind might enhance your response to medical treatment? Do you want a sense of control over recovery?

If you answered yes to any of these questions, you absolutely want to set aside 60 minutes to listen to the Introduction to Mind Over Cancer with lecturer, author Dr. Patrick Porter. You will learn everything you need to know about the mind/body connection and how your mind can set you on the right track for recovery and lasting health. The nine creative visualization processes in this series are designed to create the ultimate healing environment for mind and body.

Titles include:
- *Staying Positive in a Negative Situation*
- *Thoughts that Harm and Thoughts that Heal*
- *Using Your Most Powerful Pharmacy*
- *Life Skills for Health and Wellness*
- *Uncommon Resources for Uncommon Times*
- *The Power of Faith and Imagery*
- *Deep Sleep for Total Mind/Body Rejuvenation*
- *Set Priorities and Stay Focused on Health*
- *Relax Your Mind and Boost Your Immune System*

Call and your local Positive Changes Hypnosis® Center to ask about this exciting program, and how you can participate.

1-877-POSITIVE or PositiveChanges.com
HypnosisToGo.com

Additional Titles by Patrick K. Porter, Ph.D.

Awaken the Genius
"Mind Technology For The 21st Century"

You'll discover how to maintain a Genuine positive attitude…how to unleash your personal passion and Enthusiasm (including stories and fun-to-do exercises)…how to develop Non-stop energy and center that energy on reaching your goals…how to activate your unlimited Imagination and creativity… how to enjoy an Unending drive to succeed… and…how to experience every day what geniuses through history have enjoyed – Spontaneous intuitive breakthroughs. (Soft cover)… $21.95

Six Secrets of G.E.N.I.U.S. • *By Patrick & Cynthia Porter, Ph.D.*

Learn simple strategies to rid yourself of negative thinking…to awaken your positive attitude in every situation…and to think your way through complex or confusing challenges. (Soft cover)